P9-DUY-402

The Psychics

The Psychics

By the Editors of Time-Life Books

TIME-LIFE BOOKS, ALEXANDRIA, VIRGINIA

CONTENTS

Essay **The Power to See the Future**
7

CHAPTER 1
Into the Mind of a Murderer
24

Essay **A Mind Sleuth on the Scent**
49

Essay **Seeking an End to Despair**
58

CHAPTER 2
The Psychic Cold War
70

Essay **Hands-on Healers**
95

CHAPTER 3
Psychic Entrepreneurs
104

Essay **Mind over Matter**
131

Acknowledgments
138

Picture Credits
138

Bibliography
138

Index
140

The Power to See the Future

Persuaded by decades of study and debate—and in some cases by personal experience many people regard psychic and paranormal phenomena as undeniably real. For such believers, the next logical step is to find ways to use the powers that researchers group under the Greek letter psi. In a world rife with unknowns, an extrasensory method of revealing the truth would indeed provide a valuable advantage.

A host of psi powers—including retrocognition (awareness of past events), clairvoyance (sight that reaches beyond the range of physical vision), and psychometry (the ability to sense an object's history)—have long been called on to aid police in detective work. Attempts at clairvoyant military espionage may be even older, and the hunch that leads to a fortune in business may be another psi power in action. But although many mysteries lie in the past or at vast distances, the greatest unknown is the future, and probably the most sought-after psychic ability is that of precognition.

The following pages present recent cases alleged to have been accurate predictions, arrived at by extrasensory means and later borne out by newspaper headlines. Some involved natural disasters; others focused on political events. Some were experienced by well-known, even famous, psychics, while one came unbidden to a Cincinnati businessman. Some forecasts manifested themselves as dreams or impressions; another was felt as physical pain. But no matter how the predictors came to know what they knew, all seemed to share one thing—the ability to glimpse the future.

The Dallas Morning News

VOL. 115—NO. 54   DALLAS, TEXAS, SATURDAY, NOVEMBER 23, 1963 — 50 PAGES IN 4 SECTIONS   ★★★★   PRICE 5 CENTS

KENNEDY SLAIN ON DALLAS STREET

★ ★ ★ ★   ★ ★ ★ ★   ★ ★ ★ ★   ★ ★ ★ ★

JOHNSON BECOMES PRESIDENT

Receives Oath on Aircraft

By ROBERT E. BASKIN
Washington Bureau of The News

In a solemn and sor-

Pro-Communist Charged With Act

A sniper shot and killed President John F. Kennedy on the streets of Dallas Friday. A 24-year-old pro-Communist who once tried to defect to Russia was charged with the murder shortly

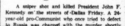

IN 1952, psychic Jeane Dixon had a chilling vision. She saw a shimmering White House with the number 1960 above it and a man near the door. A voice told Dixon that the man, a Democrat, would become president and be assassinated. Recalling this experience, in 1956 she told *Parade* magazine that a Democrat would be elected in 1960 and would die in office.

When John F. Kennedy became president in 1960, Dixon's feelings of foreboding returned, and as November 22, 1963, drew near, she tried to warn him through a former member of his inaugural committee. Friends recall Dixon saying Kennedy would die within the week, and on November 22 she said he would be killed that day. At 12:30 p.m. in Dallas her fears became fact when the president slumped over *(left),* mortally wounded by rifle fire.

While Kennedy's fate came to her in what she calls a revelation, Dixon also works with a crystal ball (below, in a 1965 portrait). A devout Catholic, she sees only divine will in her paranormal experiences. Of another accurate prediction she once said, "It was not a premonition. God showed it to me!"

"I SEE GEYSERS of water shooting in the air, and great destruction," Jeane Dixon told a friend on March 17, 1964, as they were having lunch in Washington, D.C. "It's some huge natural disaster. Up toward Canada or Alaska, very far north. I keep seeing a picture of the earth upturning, of houses breaking-up and crashing."

Then, on March 27, the strongest quake ever recorded on the North American continent ripped the frigid crust of southern Alaska. Registering 8.4 on the Richter scale, the shocks opened yawning crevices, buckled streets, and tossed houses like broken toys *(right)* on heaving slabs of frozen earth. Anchorage, a hundred miles from the epicenter, was hardest hit, but buildings toppled and people died in Valdez, Kodiak, Seward, and many other communities. Perhaps even worse than the shocks were the tidal waves, which smashed harbors from British Columbia to southern California, washing dozens of victims out to sea. Inland, severed mains spewed geysers of water, like those described by Dixon, and ruptured gas storage tanks fed fierce blazes.

Tuesday Daylight
13 Hrs. 16 Minutes
Sunrise: 9:27 a.m.
Sunset: 8:43 p.m.

Tuesday's Forecast
Cloudy
Low Tonight: 15 to 20
High Tuesday: mid 30's

Anchorage Daily Times

49TH YEAR   ANCHORAGE, ALASKA, MONDAY, MARCH 30, 1964.   PRICE 10 CENTS   IN ANCHORAGE AND VICINITY

104 FEARED DEAD IN QUAKE AREA

City Begins Major Reconstruction Task

Initial Damage Survey Reported

Anchorage, still counting limits contents at the generation losses from Friday's disastrous plant constitute the major damage to the power utility.

Mayor George Sharrock said little damage, according to Oldland. Both generators went on the line at 4 a.m. Sunday, he said.

No city utility escaped damage in the earthquake which shook the Anchorage area like a rat in the teeth of a terrier. Streets buckled and water mains burst. Power and telephone lines snapped as poles rocked in the earth tremors.

"An initial survey placed damage to city facilities alone at between $22 and $35 million," City Manager Robert Oldland said.

This figure may go much higher as crews begin repairs, he warned.

Broken down by city departments, the losses are:

Telephone. Total estimated damage was $3,125,000. There is major damage to underground cables and other parts of the outside plant. Central office equipment is partially destroyed.

Electricity. Loss of the 30,000

The city's two gas turbine generators rode the quake with little damage, according to Oldland. Both generators went on the line at 4 a.m. Sunday, he said.

Loss of the storage tank and broken power lines brought the cost of damage to Oils utility at $200,000.

Hardest hit department was public works. The water utility suffered a $7,430,000 loss. Between 20 and 30 per cent of the city's water distribution lines were almost completely destroyed. The loss from the Oils water plant into the city is a total loss. City wells were damaged.

Despite this loss, the city hopes to provide water to areas away from major breaks in the next day or two, Oldland said.

Water wagons will operate in areas without water, he said.

One quarter of the city's general collection sewers were severely damaged and the remainder were hurt to some extent. More than half of the sanitation sewers were badly damaged and the sewer lines must be replaced.

Governor Slates 8 p.m. Report On Situation

Alaskans counted 104 persons known dead or missing and presumed dead in the latest available tabulations today in the wake of the Good Friday earthquake that devastated wide sections of the central coastal areas of the state.

Damage and loss estimates were raised to half a billion dollars in a report given President Johnson by Edward McDermott, the President's personal representative who returned to Washington after an inspection of the stricken areas.

Gov. William A. Egan, at the conclusion of an emergency meeting with most of the members of his cabinet here this morning, told newsmen he had revised upwards estimates of damage inflicted by Friday's earthquake and would go on the radio at 8 p.m. today to address the public of what is being done in the emergency.

Egan said $350 million is a minimum, conservative estimate of the damage to south central Alaska. He said he expected an even greater estimate from the unknown losses of Kodiak, Valdez and Seward, led him to reassess the damage situation.

At Kodiak he had seen power barges a quarter of a mile from the closest water, most of the

"feel proud to be governor of this state and of its people," he said.

The governor said he was not yet determined whether or not there is a need for special legislation but expects in the next few days to know when the role of the legislators will be in the recovery effort.

Egan said he has discussed with Sen. E. L. Bartlett and Rep. Ralph Rivers the possibility of revising federal legislation to permit greater federal participation in natural disasters.

He said President Johnson's personal representative Edward McDermott had agreed

(Continued on Page 2)

Estimate Of City Damage $54 Million

Initial surveys of property damage in Anchorage indicate losses of $54 million, according to a damage control report.

Oldland's point out this is a rough evaluation only. First

THE TIMES

LATE LONDON EDITION
WEDNESDAY AUGUST 21 1968
NO. 57,335 SIXPENCE

Russians march into Czechoslovakia

Czechs not able to resist

By CHARLES DOUGLAS-HOME, Defence Correspondent

The Czechoslovak Army is in no position to resist an invasion of the country by its allies. The 175,000 strong force is deployed across the country with a defence from an attack from west Germany in mind, rather than an attack from the rear.

There has been no reorientation of its deployment since the change in the Prague leadership last January. One of Czechoslovakia's main difficulties during the last two months' arguments with the Russian military machine has been the fact that Czechoslovak's cannot claim to have an independent national intelligence service of her own. The intelligence service has been so closely intertwined with

PEOPLE TOLD BY PRAGUE NOT TO RESIST

Prague radio announced early today that troops of the Soviet Union, Poland and east Germany started to cross the Czechoslovak border at 11 o'clock last night without the knowledge of the Czechoslovak President, the Chairman of the National Assembly, or the First Secretary of the Communist Party of Czechoslovakia.

The Praesidium of the Czechoslovak Communist Party appealed to all people of Czechoslovakia not to resist the advancing troops and said the National Assembly and the Central Committee of the Communist Party had been called to meet to discuss the situation.

Neither the Czechoslovak Army nor the People's Militia had been called out to defend the country, the broadcast said.

IN THE AUTUMN of 1967, Czech engineer and psychic Milan Toušek *(below)* reported a vivid clairvoyant vision. He predicted that his country would be occupied by the Soviet army but that after invading, the Soviets "won't know what to do next" and would stand around in a state of idle confusion.

Sure enough, on August 20, 1968, a massive Soviet force invaded Czechoslovakia with orders to end an eight-month-old experiment in humanizing and democratizing Soviet Communism that had not even begun when Toušek made his prediction.

Party boss Alexander Dubček had suspended media censorship and allowed meetings of non-Communist political groups. Now, as occupying forces converged on Prague, Czechoslovakia's capital, they encountered not a counterrevolution but broad nonviolent resistance. Residents feigned ignorance of Russian and removed or switched street names and house numbers, making it impossible for the Soviet security police to find and arrest Czech leaders.

Confused by these measures, Soviet authorities wound up negotiating with Dubček's regime rather than crushing it. Even as the *Times* of London *(top left)* reported the crackdown, listless Soviet troops lounged outside their tanks on a Prague street *(left)*.

"SEVERE FLOODING will hit northern New Jersey and parts of New York City within two years." So wrote psychic predictor Alan Vaughan *(above)* in a list of predictions for the *National Enquirer* on May 23, 1971.

A researcher who regards precognition as "a natural function of human consciousness," Vaughan recalls that this particular prediction came to him "in stages. I had some dreams, images of water, flooding." Because he was at an early phase in the development of his predictive powers, he notes, "I didn't understand that it would cover such a huge area."

Indeed, in June of 1972 Hurricane Agnes rampaged inland, swamping much of the East Coast with record-breaking floods. Raining down an estimated 28 trillion gallons of water, the storm brought rivers over their banks in every state from Florida to Pennsylvania, killing 134 people in its ten furious days and leaving behind some $1.7 billion in damages. Among the hardest hit was the city of Wilkes-Barre, Pennsylvania *(right),* where the Susquehanna River filled the streets with twenty feet of muddy water. Wilkes-Barre is about fifty miles from the border of northern New Jersey—a near miss for psychic Vaughan—and several New York City rail roadbeds were washed out by the torrents.

Worst U.S. crash;
272 die at O'Hare

ON MAY 24, 1979, David Booth, a Cincinnati car-rental agent *(below)*, awoke in helpless tears for the tenth morning in a row. In a recurrent dream, he had stood looking up at an American Airlines plane that "wasn't making the noise it should." He watched as the jet banked off to the right, then "turned on its back and went straight down into the ground and exploded." Booth took the dream as a warning and notified the Federal Aviation Administration of a disaster he felt was imminent. But he had none of the details needed to prevent it: which plane, when, and where?

On May 25, an American Airlines DC-10 took off from Chicago's O'Hare International Airport. Soon after liftoff, the jet's left-wing engine broke loose. The crippled airliner *(far left)* rolled to the left, then plowed into the earth in a ball of flames *(near left)*, killing all 272 aboard and 3 more people on the ground. Researchers say the fact that Booth dreamed of the aircraft rolling to the opposite side is an example of mirror-image reversal often found in otherwise accurate predictive dreams. And as in Booth's dream, the plane's fatal flight was too quiet, for at least one of its engines was silent.

AS SCIENTISTS studied the rumblings of the restless Washington mountain, a woman in nearby Salem, Oregon, declared: "Mount Saint Helens will erupt in twelve hours." Twelve hours and twelve minutes later, at 8:35 a.m. on May 17, 1980, Mount Saint Helens blew up, killing some sixty people in one of the most violent eruptions *(right)* ever recorded in North America.

The woman with the uncanny forecast was Charlotte King *(above)*, who has been called a "human seismograph." King hears certain very low sounds, inaudible to other people, and feels pain just before earthquakes and volcanic eruptions. By noting the type and intensity of her symptoms—be they headaches, abdominal pain, bleeding under the skin, or what she calls "seismic flu"—King pinpoints the time and place of coming upheavals as far away as Japan and Italy.

Government scientists have found her predictions "100 percent accurate on volcanos and over 80 percent right on earthquakes." King claims no psychic gifts, but medium Ruth Montgomery believes King "was on Atlantis" when the fabled continent broke up, and learned "what the sounds were like before the catastrophes there."

Olympia Tides

Tuesday, May 20
Low 5:35 a.m., 6.4 ft.
High 9:49 a.m., 11.3 ft.
Low 4:37 p.m., .9 ft.

The Daily Olympian

The Voice Of The Capital   **A Gannett Newspaper**

Vol. 90, No. 80   **Olympia, Washington, Monday, May 19, 1980**   **Twenty-five Cents**

Olympia Weather

RAIN

Weather D3

St. Helens Blows Her Top

"I'M GETTING an impression of something structurally insecure toward the rear end of the craft. . . . it seems to be a sort of wrap-around ring . . . connected to the propulsion system. There [may be] leakage before anything more dramatic would occur. One of the components . . . is not seated properly." These were the words of psychic Beverly Jaegers *(below)* in 1981, when she was asked about the shuttle *Columbia.* Jaegers noted that her comments might apply to another shuttle. "The hardest thing to do," she says, "is pinpoint time."

On January 28, 1986, Americans watched in horror as the shuttle *Challenger,* with six scientists and a high-school teacher aboard, exploded after it left the launch pad *(right).* A presidential panel blamed the accident on the explosion of gases leaking from an improperly seated O-ring in the propulsion system near the rear of a booster rocket. NASA engineer Fred Kolb later wrote that Jaegers's "impressions were most exact and most accurate. . . . Her comment or impressions of 'leaking before anything more dramatic would occur' was exactly on target." And her impression about "improper seating [of the O-ring]," he said, "has proven to be correct."

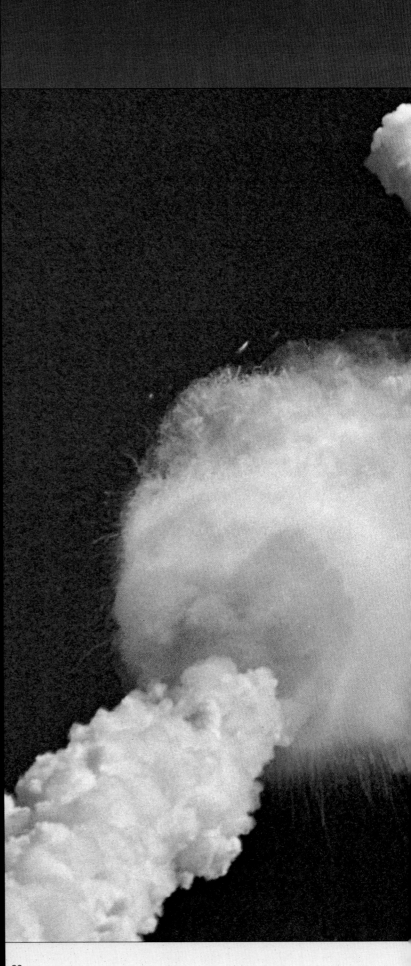

Weather
Today: Partly sunny, windy. High 58. Low 38. Wind 6-12 mph.
Saturday: Mostly sunny, windy. High 58. Wind 12-25 mph.
Yesterday: Temp. range: 56-66. AQI: 20. Details on Page B2.

The Washington Post

FINAL

Inside: Weekend
Detailed index on Page A2

112TH YEAR · · · · No. 340 · FRIDAY, NOVEMBER 10, 1989 G Prices May Vary in Areas Outside Metropolitan Washington (See Box on A2) 25¢

East Germany Opens Berlin Wall and Borders, Allowing Citizens to Travel Freely to the West

By Robert J. McCartney
Washington Post Foreign Service

EAST BERLIN, Nov. 9—Communist East Germany today opened its borders to the West, including the Berlin Wall, announcing that its citizens could travel or emigrate freely, in the most stunning step since World War II toward ending the East-West division of Europe.

Confronted by a mounting political crisis that a top East German official said has placed the ruling Communist Party's very existence at stake, the government said au-

Soviets Clear East Berlin Policy Shift

Non-Communist Rule

NOTHING SEEMED further from the realm of the possible when New York painter, author, and psychic Ingo Swann *(above)* predicted the fall of the Berlin Wall. On April 16, 1988, Swann and other well-known psychics were in the town of Dermold, in what was then West Germany, conducting a seminar on metaphysics. When some of the several hundred attendees repeatedly begged Swann for a prediction, he at last blurted out his startling forecast: The Berlin Wall, hated symbol of the Cold War partition of East and West Germany, would fall "within eighteen to twenty-four months." At the time, he felt foolish, because the Soviet Union seemed unlikely ever to relax its grip on its member nations.

But nineteen months later the East German authorities, yielding to enormous popular demands for travel rights and other freedoms, threw open the barriers to the West. As of midnight, November 9, 1989, East Germans were free to cross their borders without restriction, anywhere, even at the Berlin Wall. Swann's prediction came true that night, as East and West Berliners met atop the Wall *(left)* in a joyous all-night celebration.

CHAPTER 1

Into the Mind of a Murderer

hortly after 7:00 on the evening of April 24, 1983, twenty-eight-year-old Mary Cousett left her home in Altona, Illinois, for a night out with her boyfriend, Stanley Holliday, Jr. The couple had planned to drive to the nearby city of Peoria, but somewhere on a lonely stretch of Illinois highway, their plans went desperately wrong. Mary Cousett failed to return home that night, and no one would ever hear from her again.

Police arrested Stanley Holliday three days later in New Jersey and returned him to Illinois for questioning in connection with Cousett's disappearance. While in custody, Holliday made a shocking confession. During the drive to Peoria that night, Holliday had pulled over to the side of the road and begun arguing with Cousett. As the young man grew increasingly violent, the frightened Cousett fled from the car. Enraged, Holliday snatched up a screwdriver from his glove compartment and chased after her. Seizing her roughly by the arm, Holliday threw Mary Cousett to the ground. Then, in a blind fury, he stabbed the young woman to death.

Despite Holliday's admission of guilt, the police investigation soon hit a snag. An exhaustive search of the twenty-one miles of highway leading to Peoria failed to produce the body. Worse yet, Holliday retracted his confession, claiming that he had nothing to do with Cousett's disappearance. As the case dragged on, a local judge issued an ultimatum: The police would have to produce Mary Cousett's body or the murder charges against Stanley Holliday would be dropped. As the deadline approached, Detective William Fitzgerald, the officer in charge of the case, decided to resort to what he considered extreme measures. Setting aside his own natural skepticism, Fitzgerald placed a call to Delavan, Illinois, to the home of Greta Alexander, a professional psychic.

From the beginning of recorded history, certain gifted individuals have appeared to possess remarkable—and largely unexplained—powers of perception. Variously known as psychics, mind readers, sensitives, and intuitives, these extraordinary people display an ability to tap into knowledge and information that remain hidden to the rest of the world.

At times, this mysterious talent seems to manifest itself as clairvoyance, the ability to perceive objects and events that are beyond the range of the normal senses. At other times, an extrasensory gift might appear telepathic in nature, allowing a sensitive to divine the innermost thoughts of another person. Rarest of all, certain remarkable individuals appear to have the power of precognition, enabling them to foretell future events.

Through the ages, the men and women who seemingly possess these little-understood abilities have by turns been glorified and reviled. In a handful of societies, psychics have enjoyed an exalted status, even serving as advisers to world leaders and confidants of royalty. More commonly, however, they have operated on the shadowy fringes of society, derided as charlatans and frauds.

In recent times, a new breed of psychic has emerged, one that attempts to reconcile the mysterious world of extrasensory perception with the logic of the modern age. These psychics, many of whom consider their talent a simple fact of nature, have found ways to adapt, and even thrive, in a skeptical environment. They consult with law enforcement agencies on murders and disappearances, often sharing the thoughts and sensations of the criminal or the victim. They work in espionage, sometimes pitting their paranormal skills against the cunning of wartime enemies. Psychics have also entered the corporate arena, predicting the ups and downs of the stock market, charting a company's future, even teaching employees how to be more intuitive themselves. By finding applications for extrasensory powers, these modern psychics may one day draw back the veil of the unknown and reveal the hidden potential of the human mind.

For Illinois psychic Greta Alexander, this mysterious gift has been a potent weapon in the fight against crime. Handling more than 200 cases per year, Alexander has offered assistance to law enforcement agencies across the country, in crimes ranging from theft and fraud to kidnapping and murder. A housewife and grandmother, Alexander claims her psychic powers developed when she was a young woman, a few days after she was struck by lightning.

The disappearance of Mary Cousett provided a compelling test of Alexander's abilities. First, Detective Fitzgerald presented her with a map of the area where police had searched without success for Cousett's body. Then, while a group of police officers watched in fascination, the psychic closed her eyes and fell silent, apparently putting herself into a trancelike state. At length she began to speak, spilling out a series of seemingly nonsensical impressions while Detective Fitzgerald furiously scribbled notes.

The body of the missing woman, said Alexander, would be found on an embankment, near water. The head, she continued, would be separated from the body. A leg or a foot would also be missing. A schoolhouse would somehow figure into the scene, and the man who discovered the body would have, in her words, a "bad hand."

In all, Alexander cited more than twenty psychic impressions of the case.

here," she told the officers. The circle marked an area that police had already been over several times. Nevertheless, a fresh team renewed the search. Within three hours, their efforts were rewarded. Lying on the embankment of a river were the skeletal remains of Mary Cousett, just as Greta Alexander had described.

Many of the psychic's other impressions also proved accurate. Wild animals had scattered the young woman's bones over a wide area, so that her skull and one of her feet were separated from the body. In addition, police discovered the remains of an old schoolhouse near the spot where the body was found. Perhaps most surprisingly, the officer who discovered the body did indeed have a "bad hand." Steve Trew, an auxiliary police officer, had injured several fingers in a drill press accident some weeks earlier.

Even so, a number of police officers remained skeptical. Many of Alexander's predictions, they said, were far from convincing. She had, for instance, stated that only part of Cousett's body would be visible to the searchers and that the remains would be found somewhere near a bridge. While both of these statements proved correct, even her supporters admitted that such generalizations could simply have been good guesses. In other instances, Alexander's psychic impressions were apparently wrong. She had felt strongly that a faded highway sign would play an important role, and that tree cuttings would be found near the body. Neither prediction was accurate.

For Alexander, such quibbles were beside the point. No psychic, she insisted, is 100 percent accurate 100 percent of the time; the very nature of the phenomenon makes the results uncertain. Far more important was the final outcome. She may have been mistaken on some of the finer points of the case, but the fact remained that her psychic insights had led searchers directly to Mary Cousett's body. Having located the remains, police

When her trance appeared to be nearing its end, one of the officers present asked, "Where is the body? Can you see it?"

The psychic picked up a pencil and hesitated for a moment. Then she drew a circle on the map. "I feel the body is were able to proceed with their prosecution of Stanley Holliday, eventually obtaining a murder conviction. "I was skeptical to begin with," said Detective Fitzgerald, reviewing Alexander's involvement in the case, "but I guess I'm going to have to be a believer now."

Although most modern police investigators are slow to grasp the potential of professional psychics, the practice boasts a venerable tradition. Indeed, examples of psychics applying their skills to disappearances and murders can be found dating back to biblical times. The First Book of Samuel contains what may be the first recorded case of psychic detection. After spending three days tracking a lost herd of livestock, the shepherd Saul is about to abandon his search when his servant puts forth a strange suggestion. In a nearby land called Zuph, the servant claims, there is a mysterious seer, a holy man called Samuel. If they pay him a quarter of a shekel, Samuel will reveal the location of their lost animals. Finding the holy man at a nearby shrine, Saul is told that he should simply abandon his search for the creatures. The shepherd did as he was advised, and the entire herd reappeared, exactly as Samuel had foreseen.

By the end of the Middle Ages, it was an accepted practice for crime victims to seek the guidance of psychics, who were then commonly known as "cunning men" and "wise women." Using some methods similar to those practiced by police officials today, these adepts employed a broad range of techniques, many of which relied more on psychology than extrasensory insight, to interrogate suspects. Some wise women, for instance, practiced a skill known to modern stage magicians as "muscle reading," a technique in which unconscious body movements betray the thoughts of an unsuspecting subject. Other psychics of the era depended on methods traditionally associated with the occult, such as crystal balls and astrological charts. Even a dowser's staff could be used to apprehend wrongdoers. The seventeenth-century French writer Pierre Le Lorrain tells of a peasant whose mystical divining rod enabled him to track the murderer of a wine merchant and his wife.

With the rise of the spiritualist movement of the late nineteenth century, scientists began to devote more study to paranormal phenomena. In 1882, psychic research pioneer Frederic W. H. Myers recorded dozens of seemingly unexplainable cases of mind reading and thought transference, coining the term "telepathy" to describe them. Yet, despite the increasing acceptance of scientists, psychics found few allies in the world's law enforcement agencies.

There were some notable exceptions, however. When faced with the greatest challenge of its long history, it appears that Britain's celebrated Scotland Yard may have relied on the counsel of a psychic consultant. In 1888, a gruesome series of murders was carried out in the seedy Whitechapel district of London. Five women, many of them prostitutes, were found slain and dismembered by the demented killer known only as Jack the Ripper, whose apparent relish for his crimes shocked the city and frustrated the detectives assigned to the case. Many students of the Ripper case now believe that the beleaguered Scotland Yard was aided in its investigation by a well-known London psychic named Robert James Lees.

The author of several books on spiritualism, Lees frequently offered psychic consultations to some of London's most prominent citizens and even enjoyed the patronage of Queen Victoria herself on one occasion. He maintained an unblemished reputation as a man of integrity. Even so, Scotland Yard was reluctant to take his offers of assistance seriously. Shortly after the murders began, Lees experienced a premonition of the Ripper's next attack. Upon reporting his impressions to Scotland Yard, he was promptly turned away as a crank. When the Ripper next struck, in a pattern similar to the one anticipated by Lees, the detectives quickly dismissed the matter as a coincidence.

Nevertheless, Lees returned to Scotland Yard after having a second precognitive vision, this one involving a victim whose ears had been sliced off. This time, the Scotland Yard detectives took him more seriously; they had already received a boastful note, signed by the Ripper, in

*Turn-of-the-century spiritualists crowd the gateway to Lily Dale Assembly,
a teaching and healing community still operating today in southwestern New York.
The spiritualist movement awakened modern interest in psychic phenomena.*

which he promised to remove the ears of his next victim.

Though Lees's warning failed to prevent the next Ripper slaying, which occurred much as the psychic had foreseen, Scotland Yard was now ready to involve him in the investigation. When Lees had a third premonition, a team of constables escorted him to the location of the Ripper's latest crime. There, in the words of one witness, Lees reacted "almost like a bloodhound"; soon he was off on a chase, as if tracking a fox, through the maze of London's back streets and alleys. A short time later, Lees and his escorts found themselves standing before the door of a noted London physician. This man, declared Lees, was Jack the Ripper.

With no evidence to link the physician to the crimes of the Ripper, Scotland Yard began to make discreet inquiries. The suspect, it was learned, had been mysteriously absent from home during each of the Ripper slayings, and often displayed radical extremes of temperament—his wife described him as alternately gentle and sadistic. In time, the physician, whose identity was never revealed, was judged to be mentally incompetent by a panel of doctors and committed to an asylum for the insane. Whether or not he was guilty of any crime may never be known, but the vicious killer known as Jack the Ripper never struck again.

More than a century after the Ripper's final killing, however, the case—including the involvement of Robert Lees—remains a subject of controversy. Crime historians

are reluctant to credit the London psychic, noting that Scotland Yard continued to pursue and prosecute other suspects long after the mysterious physician was under wraps.

Although the Ripper case may never be fully laid bare, it marked a turning point in the use of professional psychics by law enforcement agencies. One man who saw great potential for psychic sleuths was Sir Arthur Conan Doyle, the creator of the fictional detective Sherlock Holmes. Doyle put his beliefs to the ultimate test when fellow crime novelist Agatha Christie mysteriously disappeared in December 1926. The episode began when Christie's car was found abandoned at the edge of a chalk pit with its motor running. The disappearance touched off a nationwide search and a flood of lurid speculation in the press. Many feared that the author had been abducted or even murdered. Scotland Yard, as it had been in so many of Christie's novels, was baffled.

Doyle firmly believed that he could locate the missing author by psychic means. For years he had been fascinated with an extrasensory talent known as psychometry, in which a physical object such as a photograph or an article of clothing is thought to serve as a conduit for

psychic vibrations and energies. Doyle had studied earlier cases in which psychometrists, upon handling an object from a crime scene, had been able to provide startlingly accurate reconstructions of the actual crimes. "It is," wrote Doyle, "a power which is elusive and uncertain, but occasionally it is remarkable in its efficiency."

Such was the case with the disappearance of Agatha Christie. With the cooperation of Christie's husband, Doyle obtained a glove that belonged to the novelist and placed it in the hands of a psychic known for his psychometric talent. "I gave him no clue at all as to what I wanted or to whom the article belonged," explained Doyle. "There was nothing to connect either it or me with the Christie case." Nevertheless, the psychic appears to have drawn a prompt impression. "There is trouble connected with this article," he told Doyle. "The person who owns it is half dazed and half purposeful. She is not dead as many think. She is alive. You will hear of her, I think, next Wednesday."

Doyle did, in fact, receive word of Christie the following Wednesday. The missing writer, who claimed to have suffered amnesia, had been found at a hotel spa, registered under an assumed name. Although the circumstances of the disappearance soon sparked controversy—some claimed that Christie had staged the affair to gain publicity—Doyle was convinced of the accuracy of the psychometrist's impressions. "Everything in the reading," he concluded, "proved to be true."

In this illustration of a biblical tale, a witch (center) summons the spirit of Samuel (right), a seer who offers Saul advice on finding his lost herd.

29

Psychometry remains a potent weapon in the arsenal of the psychic detective. The term, which means "soul measurement," was coined by Joseph Rodes Buchanan, a nineteenth-century professor of medicine at the Eclectic Medical Institute in Covington, Kentucky. In his *Manual of Psychometry,* published in 1885, Buchanan likened the skill to photographic technique. At that time, photography was largely limited to a process known as the daguerreotype, which Buchanan described as a "light painting" made by chemicals that recorded the light reflected off a subject. Buchanan believed that human beings emanated a "nerve aura" similar to this reflected light, which was transferable to inanimate objects. Psychometrists, he concluded, were simply people with an unusual sensitivity to this aura, able to read and interpret these impressions much as a daguerreotype read and interpreted light.

One of Buchanan's most enthusiastic supporters was William Denton, a professor of geology at the University of Boston. Denton's interest was piqued when he learned of a puzzling experiment conducted by George Henry Lewes, a writer and editor and the husband of famed English novelist George Eliot (the pseudonym used by Mary Ann Evans). Lewes had placed a thin wafer on a polished metal surface and then used his breath to create a layer of condensation, much like the frost of breath on a cold windowpane. When the condensation evaporated, Lewes removed the wafer and blew onto the metal again. Even though the wafer was gone, its outline could be plainly seen on the metal. The outline reappeared when Lewes returned to the experiment months later, and it could still be seen after he brushed the surface of the metal with a fine camel's-hair brush.

The experiment intrigued Denton. Perhaps, he reasoned, nature has an unknown means of recording physical events. If so, he continued, it ought to be possible—as Buchanan had suggested—for certain people to sense these impressions of the past. Denton immediately began a series of experiments, using his wife and sister as subjects. The women proved especially adept. For example, upon handling samples of handwritten letters whose authors were unknown to them, both provided accurate descriptions of the correspondents.

Denton felt convinced that he was dealing with some form of psychic phenomenon, but he was uncertain as to what type. A careful scientist, he introduced controls into his experiments. Denton believed, for instance, that many husbands and wives share what appears to be a telepathic bond. If, during the experiment with the letters, his own wife was somehow reading his mind, then what seemed to be a psychometric phenomenon might have been a telepathic one. To eliminate this possibility, Denton wrapped a selection of geological specimens in paper and then mixed them up, so that neither he nor his wife or sister knew what was inside. Denton then handed one packet to his sister. Immediately, she felt the impression of "an ocean of fire pouring over a precipice and boiling as it pours." When Professor Denton unwrapped the sample clutched in her hand, it proved to be a fragment of volcanic lava.

The results were even more impressive when Mrs. Denton handled a fragment of a mastodon's tooth. This time, she actually appeared to sense the world from the perspective of the creature itself. "I feel like a perfect monster," she reported, "with heavy legs, unwieldy head, and very large body. I go down to a shallow stream to drink. I can hardly speak, my jaws are so heavy. . . . My ears

London policemen—also known as "blue bottles"—discover a victim of Jack the Ripper lying outside a pub in this 1891 illustration (left). Scotland Yard, foiled in its attempts to stop the serial killer, is said to have resorted to the guidance of clairvoyant Robert James Lees (above, left). Lees claimed to have foreseen three of the 1888 murders and even believed he could identify the villain: He had seen Jack the Ripper in psychic visions and had then recognized him in real life, on a London omnibus. As investigators began working with Lees, Jack the Ripper mocked the seer's assistance in the case by way of a taunting note (above) sent to Scotland Yard. "You have not caught me yet you see," he wrote, "with all your cunning, with all your 'Lees,' with all your blue bottles."

Sir Arthur Conan Doyle (right), creator of the fictional detective Sherlock Holmes, developed an interest in spiritualism and psychic phenomena after his son died in World War I. When friend and fellow mystery writer Agatha Christie (above, with her collection of wooden animals from Africa) vanished in 1926, Doyle consulted British psychometrist Horace Leaf in hopes of gleaning the truth about her disappearance. Without mentioning Christie, Doyle gave the psychic one of her gloves and asked him what he perceived about its owner. Leaf immediately sensed the name "Agatha" and furnished details about her whereabouts—details that were borne out several days later when the writer turned up at a Yorkshire spa.

are very large and leathery, and I can almost fancy they flap my face as I move my head."

For Professor Denton, the science of psychometry was now a proven fact. "From the first dawn of light upon this infant globe," he declared, "nature has been busy photographing every moment." Denton went on to state that a surprising number of people possessed the ability to sense and interpret these "photographs"—one out of every ten men had psychometric talent, he declared, and four out of every ten women.

One woman who appears to have possessed this talent to an extraordinary degree was Florence Sternfels, who enjoyed a forty-year career as a professional psychometrist. Born in 1891, Sternfels lived most of her life in the small community of Edgewater, New Jersey, where she offered public readings for one dollar. Known professionally by her first name, Sternfels kept a sign on the door of her house that read simply: "Florence, Psychometrist. Walk in."

Sternfels frequently lent her talents to the police. On one occasion, she guided search teams to the body of a missing girl and also provided such a detailed description of the crime that a suspect broke down and confessed. Sternfels's ability even extended to the detection of espionage. During World War II, she alerted an army installation at Iona Island, New York, of a potential saboteur carrying dynamite in his dinner pail. The warning proved correct.

Sternfels's successes attracted a wide variety of people, including the notorious gangster Dutch Schultz, who went to Edgewater for a reading on October 21, 1935. Though put off by the gangster's rough manner, Sternfels agreed to share her impressions with him. The session ended with a stern warning: Stay out of Newark, she told him. Apparently, Schultz failed to heed the advice. Two days later, he was murdered in a Newark bar.

For the most part, Sternfels preferred to give assistance to law enforcement officials, for whom she waived her customary one-dollar fee. "As a good citizen I am glad to cooperate with these men who constantly risk their own lives to protect the public," she explained.

A psychometrist presses a glove to her brow in an attempt to discern information about the article's owner. Practitioners allegedly interpret vibrations emitted by the objects.

Thus, when the police department of Philadelphia asked Sternfels to aid in the search for two missing boys, the renowned psychic was pleased to be of service. Consulting on the case from her home in Edgewater, Sternfels produced a number of vivid impressions. Not only were the missing boys alive and well, she declared, but she could even provide the name of the street where they would be found. To the frustration of the investigating officers, however, Sternfels's information literally led nowhere; the street she had named did not exist in the city of Philadelphia.

Back in New Jersey, Sternfels remained convinced that her impressions had been accurate. Upset at what she saw as a blot on her reputation, the psychic traveled to Philadelphia at her own expense to continue the search. At City Hall, Sternfels encountered Captain George F. Richardson, the assistant chief of police for Philadelphia, who listened to her story with growing excitement. A longtime city resident, Richardson told Sternfels that she had confused her time periods; the street she had named did exist, but its name had been changed years earlier. With renewed conviction, a team of police officers escorted Sternfels to the renamed street, where the missing boys were promptly found.

Such cases brought requests for help from police departments across the United States, and from England and France. "Florence has helped police in New Jersey for over thirty years," said Edgewater's police commissioner John A. Nash in 1964. Psychic researchers were equally impressed. "I am convinced that Florence is possessed of remarkable psychic abilities," proclaimed Dr. Hereward Carrington, director of the American Psychical Institute in New York, "and of her complete honesty and sincerity."

Sternfels herself tended to brush aside such praise, and she resisted all attempts to explain her abilities in terms of spiritualism or the occult. "In fact," she once said, "if I ever saw a real ghost, I think I'd faint from sheer fright." She died on April 19, 1965, at the age of seventy-four.

While Florence Sternfels tended to shy away from the publicity her cases generated, a number of psychics, like the flamboyant Eugenie Dennis, actively sought the public spotlight. A lively and attractive woman born in Atchison, Kansas, in 1906, Dennis developed her supposed psychic talent at the age of fourteen, when she began locating lost objects for her friends and neighbors. Soon, news of her strange abilities reached the ears of famed magician David P. Abbott, who was well known for debunking the claims of fraudulent mediums and spiritualists. After four weeks of testing, Abbott was convinced that Eugenie Dennis was the genuine article. Declaring that she had a "God-given ability," Abbott encouraged the teenage psychic to embark on a tour of the United States with a theatrical company, which she did. Her performances consisted of simply answering questions posed by members of the audience.

Dennis frequently assisted police in the towns where she appeared. In Joplin, Missouri, she helped local officials track down fifteen stolen bicycles; in Chillicothe, Missouri, she led police officers to a parole violator's hideout; and in Omaha, Nebraska, she provided information that led to the recovery of twenty-three missing diamonds.

One of Dennis's most heralded cases of psychic detection—and by far the most horrific crime she had ever confronted—occurred while she was in England performing a vaudeville act. It involved a bizarre murder sensationalized in the British press as the "No. 1 Brighton Trunk crime." In June 1934, a luggage clerk at the railway station in Brighton, England, grew suspicious over an unmarked trunk that had been left unclaimed for more than a week. At last, he decided to examine the trunk's contents for a clue as to the owner's identity. A gruesome sight greeted the clerk as he pried open the lid. A female corpse, its arms and legs missing, had been roughly shoved inside.

Although the corpse in the trunk was both badly decayed and brutally dismembered, Eugenie Dennis was able to divine a great deal about the victim. Not only did she provide homicide detectives with the age and height of the woman, she also revealed that the victim was pregnant at the time of her murder, a fact later confirmed by autopsy. Then, to the horror of the investigators present, Dennis confidently declared that the murder was not an isolated occurrence; details of a related crime would soon become known. The prediction came true a few weeks later when a second corpse was discovered inside a trunk in an empty flat.

Although the Brighton trunk murders were never solved, Eugenie Dennis's testimony created a sensation. The fame of the young psychic continued to grow—at one point she even signed a three-year movie contract—and she numbered many of the era's most popular celebrities and film stars among her clients. Her remarkable career was cut short, however, on March 8, 1948, when Eugenie Dennis died in Seattle, Washington, at the age of forty-one.

Eugenie Dennis and Florence Sternfels secured only the grudging support of law enforcement officials in the United States and Europe. In other countries of the world, that support is far more readily given. In parts of Africa and Asia, where extrasensory phenomena are more widely accepted, law enforcement officials often use psychic consultants. In one famous case that occurred in the small city of Durban, South Africa, a psychic was able not only to find a

Arthur Flegenheimer—better known as underworld figure Dutch Schultz—slumps over a table in a pool of blood at the Palace Chop House & Tavern in Newark, New Jersey, in October 1935. Only two days before, Flegenheimer had visited famed psychometrist Florence Sternfels at her Edgewater, New Jersey, home for a consultation. Despite her distaste for the gangster's uncivilized demeanor, Sternfels shared her psychic impressions with him. One message that came through to her very clearly was that danger awaited Flegenheimer in Newark. She warned him to avoid the city, and had he heeded her advice, he might have lived.

murder victim's body, but also to provide her killer's motive.

On October 2, 1956, the Durban police received a report that Myrna Joy Aken, an attractive eighteen-year-old office worker known as Joy, had failed to return home from work. Questioning the young woman's colleagues, police found few leads: One co-worker thought she had seen Aken climb into a light-colored Ford Anglia after work, while another recalled that Aken had been visited on two occasions by an older man whose identity she did not reveal.

Eight days after Aken's disappearance the police had made little progress. Fearing the worst, Aken's mother and brother decided to seek the advice of a local psychic named Nelson Palmer, who was known for his skill as a psychometrist. At Palmer's request, the missing woman's mother brought along articles of her daughter's clothing. Placing the items on the table in front of him, Palmer closed his eyes and began to breathe in a measured fashion, apparently lost in contemplation. For several moments he remained

On June 17, 1934, a vile stench at the Brighton railway station (left) alerted British police to an abandoned trunk (far left) that contained the decaying torso of a young woman. Less than a month later—fulfilling a prediction by psychic Eugenie Dennis—police discovered a second trunk, this one in a basement apartment. It held the body of dancer Violette Kaye, thought to have been murdered by her boyfriend at their previous residence (below), then transported by him to a new flat, where the body was found.

still, with his hands resting on the clothing. Then, slowly, he began to speak. Joy Aken, he said, had been ruthlessly murdered; her body lay in a watery culvert. Palmer opened his eyes and stared into the face of Aken's grief-stricken mother. Although he could do little to ease her pain, he told her, he believed that he could locate her daughter's body.

At once a search party was assembled. Following Palmer's instructions, the group drove south out of the city for about sixty miles, until they neared a village called Umtwalumi. There, Palmer ordered the driver to stop the car. Climbing out, he made his way down a hillside to where a slow-moving stream of water passed through a stone culvert. Palmer peered into the culvert for a moment, then returned to the car. "You had better fetch the police," he said.

Palmer's vision had been horrifyingly accurate. Joy Aken had been shot in the head with a .22-caliber pistol and her nude, mutilated body dumped head first into the culvert. Within hours, the Durban police mobilized a force of nearly a hundred officers to track down the killer. Acting on the information from the victim's co-workers, investigators ran a check on every car in the city that matched the description of the one that had picked up Joy Aken on the day of her disappearance. Within twenty-four hours, police closed in on a radio engineer named Clarence Van Buuren, who lived only a hundred yards from the Aken family. As he was about to be apprehended, Van Buuren attempted to throw away a small, shiny object; it was a .22-caliber pistol.

Van Buuren, who had previously been imprisoned for theft and forgery, insisted that he was innocent of Joy Aken's murder. He made no secret of his acquaintance with the victim, even admitting that he had been the man who twice visited her office and gave her a lift on the day of her disappearance. According to Van Buuren, he invited Aken to join him for a drink but she refused, choosing instead to wait for him in his car while he went alone to a hotel bar. When he returned, the young woman was dead in the backseat. Realizing that he would be suspected of the crime, Van Buuren disposed of the body.

Not surprisingly, the Durban police were unconvinced

by the story. The evidence against Van Buuren was strong, and a jury found him guilty of Joy Aken's murder. Yet several officers remained troubled by the case. Although they were convinced of Van Buuren's guilt, they had failed to discover any motive for the crime.

Once again, Nelson Palmer was able to afford some insight. In an interview given to a crime reporter several years later, Palmer revealed that he had discerned more from Joy Aken's clothing than he had made known at the time. Palmer sensed that Aken and Van Buuren had been lovers and that at the time of her disappearance, she believed she was pregnant. By mutilating the body, Palmer surmised, Van Buuren hoped to destroy the signs of a pregnancy that might have incriminated him.

Palmer kept these opinions to himself during the trial, perhaps out of respect for Joy Aken's family. His reticence, however, is by no means unique. A number of psychics are reluctant to acknowledge their talent at all, much less to volunteer potentially explosive information. Often, upon coming forward with a prediction or vision, a psychic will face a backlash of disbelief and ridicule. In the cases of sensitives Etta Louise Smith and Steve Linscott, the consequences were far more serious.

On December 17, 1980, Etta Louise Smith, a thirty-two-year-old mother of two from Pacoima, California, was working in her office at a Lockheed Aircraft plant. She was listening to the radio and happened to hear a disturbing news report. Two days earlier, a young nurse named Melanie Uribe had disappeared while driving to the hospital where she worked. Until that moment, Smith had never been aware that she possessed any psychic talent, but something about the news report sparked a powerful reaction. "Mentally, somewhere, something registered," she later testified. "I saw an area. I felt this is where this person would be. I knew that it was in a canyon. My thoughts told me it was on the right-hand side."

Smith was convinced that her strange sensation had some significance, but she was reluctant to go to the police for fear, as she put it, that they would think she was "a little off my rocker." After debating the matter with herself, Smith finally decided to stop at the Los Angeles Police Department on her way home, where she told her story to Detective Lee Ryan. "I told Ryan of the news broadcast and of the vision I had had," she said. "I even drew a map on a small piece of paper." Smith told Ryan that she saw the missing nurse lying out in the open, surrounded by bushes or brush. On her hand-drawn map, she pinpointed a nearby area known as Lopez Canyon.

Although Detective Ryan promised to send a search party to the canyon, Smith feared the police had not taken her seriously. That night, along with her two children, she resolved to investigate the matter herself.

A drive through Lopez Canyon revealed nothing, and Smith began to wonder if she had made a foolish mistake. Then, on the way back, "I started getting queasy," she said. "I had terrible vibes." Just then, Smith's daughter spotted something in the distance; several hundred yards off was a white object surrounded by shrubs and brush. As they walked toward the object, Smith's eyes focused on a pair of white shoes. "When I saw the shoes I said, 'Oh, my God. Those are white nurse's shoes. It's got to be her.' " The trio flagged down a police officer, reported what they had seen, then returned home.

Within moments, two police officers appeared at the door. Acknowledging Smith's help in the case, they asked her to return to the station, simply to "fill in the blanks." Once they had arrived at the police station, however, the tone of their questioning grew increasingly hostile. Again and again, the officers demanded to know how Smith had been able to track down the body. They refused to believe that she had experienced a psychic vision. Although Smith had freely volunteered her information, the police seemed to suspect her of some form of complicity in the crime.

The questioning dragged on past midnight. Finally, Smith was asked to submit to a lie detector test; she readily agreed. "I don't have anything to hide," she told the officers. The Los Angeles police felt otherwise. While sensors measured her pulse rate and other bodily reactions, a polygraph operator posed a series of blunt questions.

"Did anyone tell you they killed the woman before you went to the police?" the examiner asked.

"No," answered Smith.

"Were you present when she was killed?"

"No," she answered again.

By the time the examination ended, Smith was badly flustered and the detectives who had been questioning her had grown even more antagonistic. "I asked how my polygraph went," she recalled. "One of them said, 'Are you kidding? You failed it.' He said I was a damn liar."

At 5:00 the following morning, after more than seven hours of interrogation, Etta Louise Smith was formally charged with the murder of Melanie Uribe. Obviously the officers involved had little use for psychic intuition and therefore refused to credit Smith's story. In addition, it is well known that certain types of criminals often come forward with information about their own cases, almost daring the police to catch them. But in a purely objective examination of the Melanie Uribe murder, the accusations against Etta Louise Smith seem preposterous. The young woman had not only been brutally slain but also sexually assaulted—making Smith an unlikely suspect. Nevertheless, the Los Angeles police clearly felt she had been an accomplice.

After four days in jail, however, Smith was released; three young men had been arrested in connection with the case. In time, they would be convicted of the murder.

During the same year, a twenty-six-year-old Bible student from Oak Park, Illinois, became caught up in a similar case. In early October 1980, Steve Linscott was asleep in his home alongside his wife when he had a troubling dream. "A man is talking with somebody in a conversational manner," he later recalled, trying to reconstruct the events of his dream. "They talk for a bit, and then space changes. There seemed to be a very evil intention to this person, and he pulled a short, blunt object from behind his back or from somewhere behind him, and displays that to whoever he's talking to. I woke up at that point, and when I went back to sleep, sometime during the night, I resumed, apparently, the same dream. This time, this person was now standing over somebody, beating somebody very violently. All I really could see in this part of the dream was kind of a silhouette of this person cracking down on somebody and blood flowing. I guess this somewhat frightened me at the time, and I woke up."

That same night, in an assault shockingly similar to Linscott's dream, a young nursing student named Karen Phillips was beaten to death with a blunt metal object less than half a block from the Linscotts' home. Linscott was stunned when he learned of the crime from police officers who were canvassing the neighborhood. After discussing his dream with his wife, he decided to report it to the police. Linscott spent three hours at the Oak Park police station, describing his dream in detail for a number of officers.

Two days later, the police asked Linscott to return for more questioning, telling him that his dream was their only lead. By now, Linscott had grown apprehensive and asked outright if they suspected him of the crime. The police assured him that they did not, but that they needed to eliminate him as a suspect in the event that his testimony was required in court. Reassured, Linscott voluntarily donated samples of his hair, blood, and saliva for forensic testing.

As in the case of Etta Louise Smith, the police grew increasingly aggressive as the interrogation dragged on. Exhausted, Linscott took one of the officers aside and demanded to know why he was being questioned so carefully. The reply shocked him. "My partner and I and everyone else is convinced you killed this young lady," the officer told him. "The evidence that you gave us tonight will convict you. . . . You walk out of this door, and when we come back and arrest you, you will get the electric chair."

The officer's accusation was not without foundation. Although Linscott had passed a lie detector test, the hair samples he had freely given were found to match those

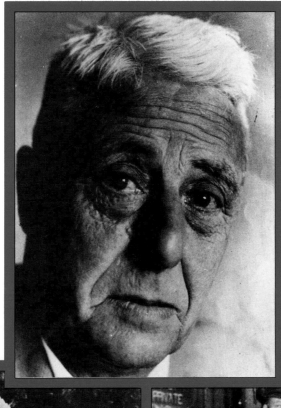

A smiling bridesmaid (below) on her friend's wedding day, Myrna Joy Aken disappeared shortly thereafter, prompting the family of the eighteen-year-old South African girl to contact a local psychometrist. Nelson Palmer (right), a sixty-three-year-old retired headmaster of a nearby school, needed only to touch a few pieces of Aken's lingerie to fall into a clairvoyant trance. He accurately sensed that the young woman had been murdered, and he disclosed the whereabouts of her body. Clarence Van Buuren, pictured below in police custody, was hanged for the crime in 1957.

recovered from the victim's apartment. On November 25, seven weeks after the murder of Karen Phillips, Steve Linscott was arrested and charged with murder. In prosecuting their case, police asserted that what Linscott described as a dream was actually an admission of guilt, the confession of a possibly schizophrenic killer. One dream expert even theorized that Linscott was some sort of sleepwalking murderer. In the end, the prosecution concentrated on physical evidence, notably the hair samples discovered in Phillips's apartment. Though legally inconclusive, the evidence apparently convinced the jury. Linscott was convicted of first-degree murder and sentenced to forty years in prison.

The case remains highly controversial. In 1983, Linscott's conviction was overturned by the Illinois State Court of Appeals, but six months later the state supreme court upheld the guilty verdict, stating that Linscott's dream contained "unusual details which correlated with the actual murder" and that the forensic analysis of Linscott's hair, "while not conclusive in itself, nonetheless provides additional support to the jury's verdict."

Forensic Psi

When a human skeleton was uncovered in Columbia, Maryland, on December 15, 1975, officials called on anthropologist J. Lawrence Angel and police artist Donald Cherry to help identify the body. Angel determined that the skull belonged to a caucasian female about twenty years old. It was left to Cherry to fill in the details. Cherry *(above)* is not your typical police artist. Reluctant at first to call himself psychic, he concedes that he does receive mental images of his subjects. As Washington, D.C.'s first full-time police artist—he is now retired—Cherry spent his days interviewing victims and sketching the likenesses of alleged perpetrators. Relaxing the victims with friendly conversation, he developed a rapport with them. "I've got to get them on my side first," he explained, "or we never get anyplace." As they talked, Cherry would envision the criminal. "All of a sudden, the picture begins to draw itself. It starts to become somebody."

In the case of the skull found by the Maryland police *(right),* Cherry perceived a woman with a long face and gently sloping eyes *(center).* After running his sketch in a local paper, three readers identified the woman as Roseanne Michele Sturtz *(far right).* Her murderer remains at large.

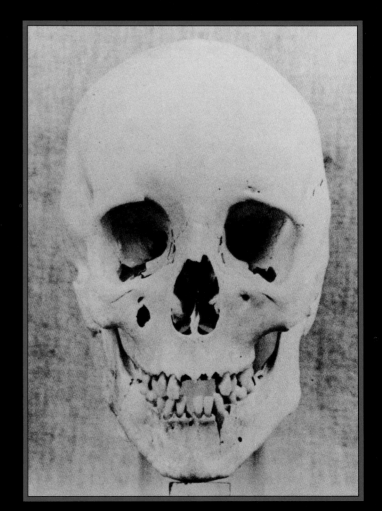

In all likelihood, the truth in the Steve Linscott case will never be known, but the affair raises a number of troubling questions. Although Linscott was not a professional psychic—in fact, he had never before reported any extra-sensory experience—his fate could easily have befallen Greta Alexander or Florence Sternfels before their reputations became so well established.

While few expect to be imprisoned the way Steve Linscott or Etta Louise Smith was, some psychics shy away from openly touting their skills in such a highly skeptical society. Psychics, almost by definition, are outsiders, and their talents often subject them to unwanted scrutiny. In addition, no psychic has complete control over his or her abilities; in many instances, the visions and impressions come without warning—or not at all. For those who depend on their talents to earn a living, a widely publicized failure can bring considerable damage.

Given the almost arbitrary nature of most psychic phenomena, the case of Chicago psychic Irene Hughes seems all the more extraordinary. Not only did she test her talent against a highly volatile political intrigue, she did so before a live radio audience. On October 5, 1970, the whole of Canada was shocked when a pair of high-ranking government officials—British Trade Commissioner James Jasper Cross and Quebec Labor Minister Pierre LaPorte—were kidnapped by a radical terrorist group known as the F.L.Q., or Front de Liberation du Quebec. The terrorists, who had previously bombed several public buildings, demanded the immediate release from jail of twenty-three members of their group, whom they termed "political prisoners." Canadian officials quickly entered into negotiations, but they held out little hope of reaching a peaceful solution. The prospects for the captured men appeared bleak.

On October 14, Canadian broadcast-journalist Robert Cummings, the host of a radio talk show called "Afterthought," placed an on-air telephone call to American psychic Irene Hughes at her home in Chicago. Hughes, who had previously gained notoriety for predicting the launchpad explosion of the *Apollo 1* spacecraft, was unfamiliar with the details of the kidnapping when she received

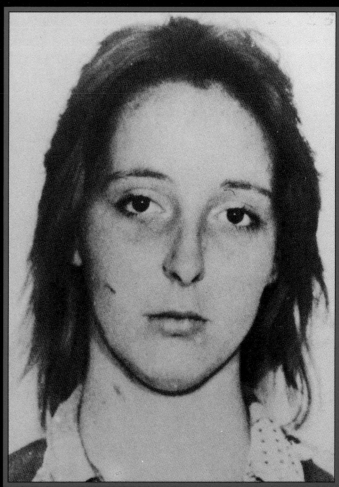

When, in early October 1970, two Canadian officials were abducted by a Quebec separatist terrorist group, the Canadian public was transfixed by the news. Those who turned their radios to the syndicated talk show hosted by Robert Cummings heard the first of several interviews held with Chicago psychic Irene Hughes (top left). Hughes accurately described the terrorists' hideout in northwest Montreal (far left) and predicted that British Trade Commissioner Jasper Cross, shown at left in a photograph taken by his captors, would come to "no physical harm." When asked about Labor Minister Pierre LaPorte (top right), Hughes was less optimistic; she believed his life was in danger. Although she did not mention it at the time, Hughes later claimed to have had an impression of a green automobile. On October 17, LaPorte's lifeless body was found in the trunk of a green Chevrolet (above).

Cummings's call. Nevertheless, following a brief explanation of the situation, Hughes made an astonishingly precise and decisive series of predictions. James Cross, she told the audience, was alive and unharmed, and would remain so. She was less optimistic regarding Pierre LaPorte. When pressed repeatedly, Irene Hughes admitted that she believed LaPorte's life was in jeopardy. Before concluding the interview, Hughes also predicted that an arrest would come quickly, and that on November 6, there would be a "striking and unusual" development in the case.

On October 17, the body of Pierre LaPorte was discovered in the trunk of a green Chevrolet abandoned at a military base. He had been both strangled and stabbed. The following day, Robert Cummings again called Irene Hughes. After expressing her dismay over the death of LaPorte, the psychic rebuked herself. During their earlier conversation, she said, she had experienced an odd impression of a green automobile, but thought it unimportant. She then repeated her conviction that James Cross was still alive.

Cummings, impressed by the uncanny accuracy of the psychic's earlier predictions, pressed her to reveal the exact location where James Cross was being held. Once again, Hughes gave a startlingly detailed answer. "I will say five miles northwest of Montreal," she said. "It seems that the place he is in is about three stories high. I feel that it is red brick, a kind of old place, and it actually could be an apartment building."

No sooner had Cummings completed his broadcast than he contacted the authorities, but their response was lukewarm. Not only were the officials involved in the case reluctant to ally themselves with a psychic, they went so far as to instruct Cummings to discontinue his live broadcasts, presumably because they posed a threat to the investigation. Cummings complied, but he continued to record his private conversations with Irene Hughes and to make transcripts available to the authorities.

On November 6—the date on which Hughes had predicted "striking and unusual news"—police arrested one of the kidnappers in West Montreal. The same day, authorities confirmed that they had received an authentic recent photograph of James Cross seated on a box of explosives.

Following the arrest, the kidnapping plot quickly came unraveled. Within a month, James Cross was freed by his captors. Upon Cross's release, the remarkable accuracy of Hughes's predictions soon became a matter of public record. Cross had been held for sixty days in a three-story, red-brick apartment building in a northwest suburb of Montreal, exactly as Hughes had stated.

"My mind almost boggles when I consider the remarkable accuracy and detail of Irene's many psychic evaluations," said Robert Cummings at the conclusion of the case. "There were predictions of major consequence, such as the events of November 6 and Cross's release; her accurate description of the LaPorte kidnappers' automobile and the three-story brick duplex northwest of Montreal where Cross was held. Undoubtedly, this endeavor represents an impressive documentation of ESP at work in a 'now' manner in modern history."

Not all psychics have been so successful in applying their talent to newsworthy crimes. In at least two well-known cases—the 1974 kidnapping of Patty Hearst, heiress to the Hearst publishing empire, and the 1980 Atlanta child murders—an otherwise accomplished psychic named Dorothy Allison found herself completely stumped. The failures were decidedly uncharacteristic. Allison, a homemaker from Nutley, New Jersey, has collected scrapbooks of newspaper clippings attesting to her success at solving crimes and locating missing persons. In addition, she has amassed a large collection of police badges and a bulging sheaf of testimonials to her skill from grateful police investigators. In cases of homicide, she says, her psychic powers enable her to experience the crime from the killer's point of view. "What I do," she says, "is hop on the killer and stick with him every minute of his life."

Although she does not accept payment for her services, Allison pursues her craft with the zeal of a devoted professional. "I work eighteen hours a day, and I work on many cases at one time," she says. "I'm out to get killers 100 percent and I want to smack their faces."

The case of Patty Hearst, one of the most notorious kidnapping cases in modern history, pushed Dorothy Allison's skills to their limit. Her involvement began on February 8, 1974, when she received a call from Randolph Hearst, the abducted woman's father. Hearst had reservations about consulting a psychic, but Allison soon impressed him by accurately describing, over the telephone, the contents of the room in which he was sitting. That same day, Hearst flew her out to San Francisco.

For three days, Allison toured San Francisco's Bay Area attempting to use her psychic sense to home in on the missing heiress. Although she failed to locate Patty Hearst, over the course of her involvement with the celebrated case Allison made a number of predictions that subsequently proved to be true. Allison told Randolph Hearst that his daughter was being held in a closet-size cell against her will. Eventually, the psychic continued, Patty would be captured alive and well. Prior to that, however, she would dye her hair red and travel freely across the country.

Each of these predictions was eventually borne out. "Dorothy couldn't locate Patty, but I think she is an honest and reputable woman," Randolph Hearst later declared. "I guess you could call me a semibeliever."

Despite her mixed results in the Hearst case, Dorothy Allison's reputation continued to grow. In October 1980, she was invited to Atlanta, Georgia, to assist in the hunt for a brutal serial killer. For eighteen months, the city of Atlanta had been held in a grip of terror as eighteen children were abducted and murdered. The entire nation had watched the tragedy unfold with increasing horror and frustration, and with each crime, the killer continued to elude the police.

Dorothy Allison arrived in Atlanta amid a swirl of controversy. No sooner had she stepped off the airplane than she was surrounded by a cluster of newspaper and television reporters. Uncomfortable in the media spotlight, Allison nonetheless took the opportunity to boldly assure the people of Atlanta. "I can guarantee he won't murder while I'm here," she stated flatly. "I will control him. I have seen who he is. I see where he is. I follow him."

Despite her bravado, Allison's only correct prediction in the Atlanta child murders was to identify the killer as a black male. Later, after the alleged killer—a black male named Wayne Williams—was arrested, Allison insisted that she had given the police the name Williams over the course of her consultations. The claim was flatly denied by Atlanta's chief of police.

For the skeptical, such failures only confirm their doubts about the wisdom of employing psychics to investigate crimes. Critics of the practice contend that turning to psychics may actually hinder the police in many cases. People like Dorothy Allison, they say, divert the resources of the police from the more conventional investigative methods, often to no benefit. A police detective named George Brejack would probably agree. Brejack stated in a 1980 interview with a New York television station that Dorothy Allison showed up at the Paterson, New Jersey, police headquarters one day uninvited—something she claims never to do—and offered to help with the case of a missing eight-year-old boy. Brejack accepted her help, although he came to regret it. "She was in for seven days," he explained, "but she kept making wrong predictions. We went all over the place with her; we even had fire trucks pump out an old building full of water because of her. Then she disappeared. Two weeks later, the body was found, clear on the other side of town from where she said."

According to Brejack, when the discovery of the body hit the news, Allison called asking for a letter on department stationery confirming her contribution. Brejack refused. Allison chalked it up to professional jealousy.

The famed magician James Randi, who has devoted much of his career to debunking the claims of psychics and spiritualists, is among those critics who argue that psychics are often quick to claim credit for solving cases, as Allison

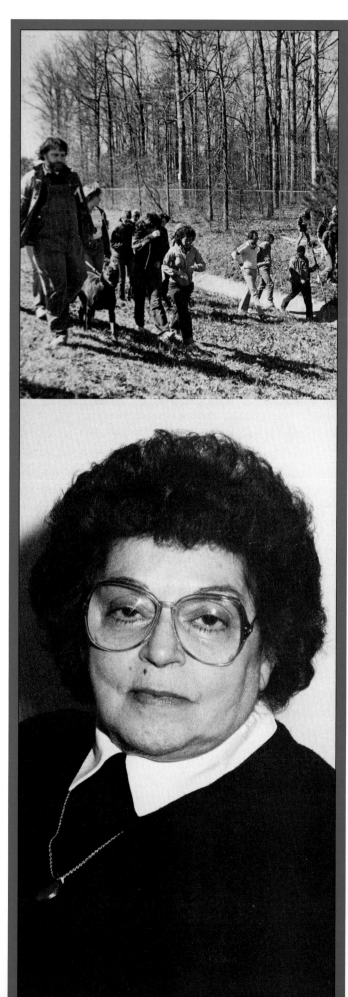

allegedly did, when in truth they have provided little more than vague impressions and predictions. He strongly opposes the use of psychics in police work. "Until police departments reject these charlatans as publicity-seeking clowns," he declares, "the so-called 'psychic detectives' will continue to interfere with effective police work and profit from the glory they borrow from such official association."

Not everyone shares this harsh assessment, however. "I have the philosophy that I don't care who solves a case as long as it gets solved," says Sergeant Joseph Perkins, a Connecticut police officer who has worked with psychics on occasion. "I've gone in closets with them and looked at candles. I put my head in a paper bag and looked for ghosts. . . . Yet I still listen to them because someday one might come up with something." Some police departments across the United States share Sergeant Perkins's sentiments—a number are beginning to develop official guidelines to govern and regulate the use of psychic consultants.

In much the same spirit, a St. Louis psychic named Beverly Jaegers has launched an effort to impose an orderly system on the practice of psychic detection. In 1971, Jaegers founded the Psychic Detective Bureau, also known as the Psi Squad. Drawing on her skills as both a psychic and a licensed private investigator, Jaegers has attempted to establish a national network of psychics that can pool its resources to assist police more effectively than ever before. Jaegers hopes that her approach will dispel some of the misconceptions about psychic phenomena. "Psychic abilities are something we all have and can develop," she says. "They are not 'gifts' and they are not 'powers.' "

Whether gift, power, or innate ability, reaching beyond the normal senses has its price, particularly in cases of violent crime. "It's dangerous," says New Jersey psychic Nancy Czetli, who has assisted in more than 200 investigations. "You are asking a highly sensitive instrument, essentially, to put itself through what the victim went through. And you have to do that without losing your mind."

Unlike Dorothy Allison, who claims to experience her

Psychometrics 101

According to St. Louis psychic Beverly Jaegers, psychic powers are within the reach of everyone. These extraordinary forces are just extensions of the five normal senses, she believes, and even beginners can tap their psychic potential by patiently following the exercises she outlines in her 1974 book, *Practical ESP and Clairvoyance.*

To start, Jaegers recommends practicing visualization, which helps you learn to see with the mind's eye. First, relax and close your eyes. Now summon the image of a daisy. Try to see its colors, size, and shape. Create a complete mental picture. Then visualize the outside of your home, in great detail.

Next, work on what Jaegers deems one of the simplest of psychic skills, psychometry. The goal is to teach your hand to become a third eye; practicing color sensitivity, she says, is the first step.

Pick up some paint sample cards in primary colors—red, yellow, blue. Clip out the individual colors and paste each on its own white index card. Then, relax. Place the red card face up on a table in front of you. Using the hand you do not write with, run your fingertips over the color. Try to sense the texture of the color, not the card. Then do the same with the blue card. It should feel different.

If you do not succeed immediately, do not despair. Jaegers says that most people need to practice for quite a while. Work with two colors until you are getting consistent sensations from each. Then close your eyes and try to tell the two apart by feel. As your confidence grows, add colors. Then branch out. Obtain a deck of playing cards with blank backs so you can feel the colors of the cards when they are lying face down. Learn to tell red from black and suit from suit. Use psychometry to identify pictures in envelopes or objects in a box. Above all, keep practicing.

cases from the criminal's point of view, Nancy Czetli generally adopts the perspective of the victim. "What I try to do is link my mind with the victim's," she says. "I don't become the victim, but it's as if I'm standing alongside him. The victim's brain, even if the person is dead, contains a residue of thought pattern, and I tap into that—even details that are stored in the victim's subconscious."

In the case of Leonetta Schilling, a sixty-two-year-old woman who was stabbed to death in her home in Riviera Beach, Maryland, this perspective proved especially harrowing. On June 8, 1979, Schilling's husband found his wife lying in a pool of blood on their kitchen floor. She had been stabbed eleven times.

Mrs. Schilling died on the way to the hospital, leaving police with no clues to her assailant's identity. In a month's time, detectives assigned to the case had compiled a list of thirty-two possible suspects but could find no firm evidence against any of them. Fearing that the trail was growing cold, they enlisted Nancy Czetli's aid.

"I began to build a feeling for the assailant and his relationship to Mrs. Schilling," Czetli later recalled. "I knew that he abused drugs, and also that he knew his victim very well. In fact, I told the police that Mrs. Schilling was not afraid of her killer—she had been his baby sitter." Studying the case further, Czetli took her impressions to another level. "I was able to visualize the confrontation," she reports. "When the murderer demanded money from Mrs. Schilling, she refused to give it to him. Then she proceeded to give him a severe dressing down, to which he reacted violently."

Nancy Czetli's psychic reconstruction of the crime enabled her to provide a detailed description of the killer, whom she believed to be a slightly built, fair-haired carpenter. When the police showed her photographs of their numerous suspects, the psychic focused in without hesita-

As members of the U.S. Psi Squad look on, founder Beverly Jaegers opens a package of bullets removed from the body of a Mississippi murder victim in 1974. The group—a licensed detective agency—uses psychometry and other psychic skills to aid law enforcement officials in investigations.

tion. Pointing to one of the likenesses, she declared, "This man's thought pattern is most similar to that of the killer's." The picture was that of Allen Finke, Leonetta Schilling's twenty-six-year-old nephew. As Nancy Czetli had claimed, the victim had no reason to fear her killer—she had, in fact, often looked after him when he was a child.

Within a week, police had arrested Finke, who was subsequently convicted of murder and sentenced to life imprisonment. "It would have taken us six months to get statements from those thirty-two suspects and then verify their alibis," said Sergeant James Moore, one of the officers assigned to the case. "Finke was way down at the bottom of our list. We wouldn't have gotten to him for months, and by that time who knows where he might have gone?"

As with Nancy Czetli and Dorothy Allison, California psychic Dixie Yeterian employs her talent to reexperience a crime, often with horrifying results. Yeterian, who frequently aids local police in cases of missing persons and homicide, was left badly shaken on one occasion when her abilities took her deep into the mind of a vicious killer.

In 1978, while conducting a radio call-in show, Yeterian received a call from a distraught teenager named Tom Eldridge. "My father has disappeared," the young man told her. "I want to know if you can help me find him." Yeterian told the boy to bring a photograph of his father to the radio station, along with an assortment of personal belongings. By the time the psychic had finished her program, Eldridge had arrived at the studio. Obviously agitated, the young man handed her a watch and a ring that belonged to his father. The psychic took the objects and promised to call as soon as she had received any psychometric impressions.

Returning home, Yeterian placed the watch and ring on a table and began to concentrate. A flood of haunting images now swirled before her eyes. At first, she saw a random pattern of objects: a chain-link fence, a boat, a wrench, and a rifle. Then, to her horror, the disjointed objects resolved themselves into a gruesome scenario.

Tom Eldridge, the psychic saw, had been lying when he approached her at the radio station. The young man's

Pennsylvania psychic Nancy Czetli searches an open field in 1988 for the body of a murder victim. Czetli receives such detailed images of murder sites, she knows that "if every element in my vision isn't there, the place isn't the right one." She was unable to find the body of this victim but did help police in other aspects of the case.

show of concern over his father's supposed disappearance, it seemed, had been a ruse to divert suspicion from himself. In truth, the young man had quarreled violently with his father earlier that day and then—in a moment of uncontrolled fury—shot him in the head with a rifle.

"I felt Tom's emotions, or rather, lack of emotion," Yeterian recalled. "He was totally cold when he pulled that trigger, filled with rage that went beyond feeling. It wasn't just the result of their argument. It went all the way back to his infancy. It was an accumulation of frustrations. The kind of frustrations that come from being a child at the mercy of a brutal adult. He'd been beaten, humiliated, dehumanized. Lately, he'd begun to argue back. But he'd never won an argument. How could he win an argument with his father? Their confrontations always ended with the impact of his father's fist."

Almost in spite of herself, Yeterian clearly saw the blast of the rifle as the drama played out in her mind. "Tom watched his father crumple to the ground," she declared. "Then he went to the bed, pulled off a white bedspread, went out, and wrapped his father up in it. There was no emotion in his actions. Just cool precision. He put the body in the back of a camper truck, drove the truck east of town, onto a country road, then carried his father's body up a steep hill, where he buried it."

As her perceptions drew her deeper into the horrible scene, Yeterian was surprised to find herself shifting perspective from Tom's point of view to that of his murdered father, a phenomenon she later described as a "psychic split." Now, as the scene continued in her mind, she actually experienced the sensations of the dead man.

"I felt the blow as the bullet hit his head, and the sick, wilting feeling that followed. I knew he was wrapped in the white bedspread because he saw it being wrapped around him. When I saw the green carpet on the camper floor, I saw it through the dead man's eyes. As I concentrated on him, I felt his sensations as Tom carried him up the hill. I watched through his eyes as his son dug a grave."

Only then, as she watched Tom Eldridge through his dead father's eyes, did Yeterian begin to understand the true depth of the young man's rage. Simply murdering his father had not been enough. Now, as he prepared the older man's grave, Tom Eldridge carried out a shocking series of atrocities. "Tom castrated his father," Yeterian said. "He made a cross with sticks, placed it over his father's heart and urinated on it. In the frenzy of his hatred, he tied a green cloth around his father's throat and strangled him, although his father was already dead."

Within an hour of receiving the watch and ring from Tom Eldridge, Dixie Yeterian placed a call to Del Romanos, a homicide detective with whom she had previously worked. Later that day, Romanos picked up Tom Eldridge and confronted him with the grisly details gleaned by Yeterian. Stunned by the accuracy of the information, the young man broke down and confessed to the murder of his father.

Eldridge's confession was not the only confirmation of Dixie Yeterian's vision. Once the body had been recovered, police were able to verify that each one of the graphic details she had provided was correct in every particular.

Despite Dixie Yeterian's outstanding success, the police remained close-mouthed about her involvement in the case. During a press conference the following day, Detective Romanos would say only that "intuition" had led them to suspect Tom Eldridge in the murder of his father.

The world of law enforcement may never fully accept the possibilities afforded by psychic phenomena, despite the accomplishments of people like Dixie Yeterian. This resistance, according to psychic Beverly Jaegers, stems from a simple misunderstanding of the nature of these abilities. Psychic power, she insists, is neither mysterious nor rare. Rather, it is an acquired skill, available to anyone. Toward that end, Jaegers's Psi Squad offers counsel and training to all who are interested, in the hope of reaching a greater understanding of how these strange abilities work.

"The mind is capable of rather amazing things," Jaegers says matter-of-factly. "And all I'm saying is, having discovered that these things are possible, we're trying to find out how they're done. Take it or leave it."

A Mind Sleuth on the Scent

Everybody has psychic ability," says Texas psychic detective John Catchings, who began developing his own uncanny powers after he was struck by lightning at a July 4 barbecue in 1969. People remain unaware of their paranormal potential, he says, because society "teaches us to think in purely logical terms; if something illogical occurs to us, we reject it. I have disciplined myself to pay attention to those thoughts."

Using his abilities to solve crimes is a full-time occupation for Catchings, whose clients credit him with dozens of successes, from discovering the body of a murdered teenager to finding a gold medal taken from the body of another crime victim. Although critics argue that Catchings owes his results to common-sense deduction rather than psychic insight, others believe only psi powers can account for what he is able to do. "At first I thought it was weird," says Detective Ronald Roark of the Ennis, Texas, police department, who has worked with Catchings. "Now I feel that someday psychics will be part of all larger police departments—it's another tool of the trade, like fingerprinting or photographing."

Catchings himself takes a similarly pragmatic view of his mysterious talent. "About twenty percent of the time I'm dead wrong," he admits. "Another sixty percent I'm only partially right. But on the last twenty percent, I'm right on it." The following pages depict a prime example of that successful twenty percent: the Texas psychic's crucial role in solving the disappearance of a young Houston woman named Gail Lorke.

Outward appearances would have suggested that thirty-two-year-old Gail Lorke had a fine life. A vibrant, pretty woman, she enjoyed her work as a nurse in Houston, and she and her husband Steven shared a passion for country music and dancing.

But on October 29, 1982, Gail Lorke vanished. A week later, Steven Lorke told police that the night before his wife disappeared they had gone square-dancing—as visualized at right by an artist—and that the next morning she felt too ill to go to work. "When I came home that evening, she was gone," Lorke said, "I haven't seen her since." He said he had not reported her disappearance earlier because he thought that she had walked out on him but that she would return.

Police investigators learned Gail's life was not as idyllic as it appeared. According to her husband, the missing woman abused drugs, wrote bad checks, and may have had a lover. The Lorkes' relationship was so strained that they had divorced a few years earlier, only to remarry.

The police concluded Gail had simply fled a bad marriage. But her sister, Marty Wing, did not agree. She believed Gail had been murdered by Steven Lorke.

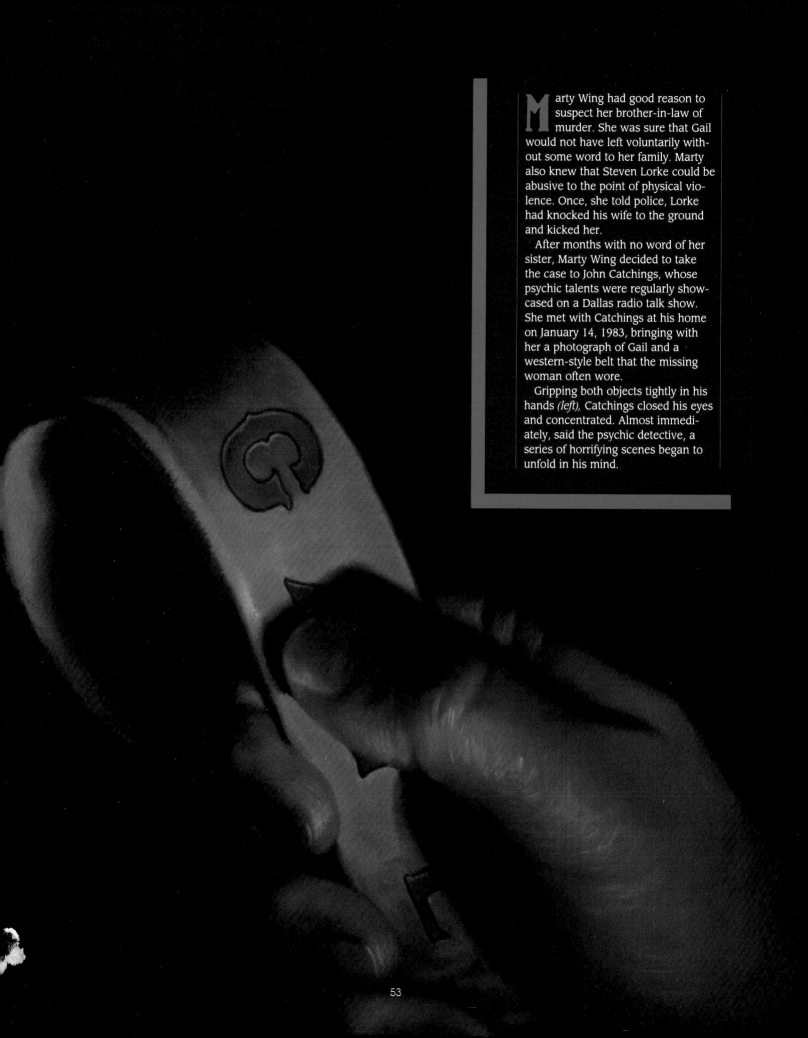

Marty Wing had good reason to suspect her brother-in-law of murder. She was sure that Gail would not have left voluntarily without some word to her family. Marty also knew that Steven Lorke could be abusive to the point of physical violence. Once, she told police, Lorke had knocked his wife to the ground and kicked her.

After months with no word of her sister, Marty Wing decided to take the case to John Catchings, whose psychic talents were regularly showcased on a Dallas radio talk show. She met with Catchings at his home on January 14, 1983, bringing with her a photograph of Gail and a western-style belt that the missing woman often wore.

Gripping both objects tightly in his hands *(left)*, Catchings closed his eyes and concentrated. Almost immediately, said the psychic detective, a series of horrifying scenes began to unfold in his mind.

Catchings says that as he held Gail Lorke's belt and photograph, he could see what seemed to be key events from the night she disappeared—scenes that did not match Steven Lorke's story. That evening, as Catchings saw it, Gail and Steven had begun fighting as soon as they got home from a square-dancing class. Steven accused his wife of flirting with other men. In the vision, Steven's anger erupted into violence. With a wild cry, he seized Gail's neck, gripping her with such convulsive strength that he snapped her spine *(far left)*.

To hide the evidence, Catchings continued, Steven took the corpse to a field and left it partly covered with trash, dirt, and something "big and white" *(above)*. Catchings also sensed a well or other water in the area. Later, according to Catchings, the remorseful husband returned several times to the grave. Soon that secret would prove to be Steven's undoing.

Urged on by Catchings, Marty Wing contacted Detective Ronald Phillips of the Harris County Sheriff's Department. Though skeptical, Phillips agreed that Steven Lorke made a plausible suspect and brought him in for questioning.

But Lorke calmly stuck to his story, even agreeing to a polygraph test. Frustrated, Phillips decided to gamble on Catchings's vision. He asserted that police knew Lorke had made furtive visits to his wife's grave site.

Perhaps believing he had been observed, Steven cracked. He confessed to his wife's murder and led police to the body. In a scene much like the one Catchings had described *(right),* police found the remains of Gail Lorke hidden beneath a pile of trash and sections of light-colored picket fence. Nearby, a flap attached to a fire hydrant was stamped with the word "well."

felt it was baloney at first," Phillips said of Catchings and other psychic detectives. "He made me believe in them. They've got a power there— it gives you goose bumps."

During the 1920s and 1930s, Germany was home to more astrologers per square mile than any other nation. One of them was Elsbeth Ebertin (right), who wrote popular almanacs of prophecy.

In 1923 Ebertin made several predictions about Adolf Hitler (above, saluting the Nazi party's private army in 1927). Her book *A Look into the Future* (far right) asserted that the then-Nazi chief would rise to still greater power but that he was likely to "expose himself to personal danger by excessively uncautious action."

Believers saw Ebertin's words come true during the Beer Hall Putsch in Munich that November. Hitler and other Nazis attempted to launch an overthrow of the government by rabble-rousing at a political meeting being held at the Bürgerbräu beer cellar. In a skirmish between police and the Nazis, Hitler fell and broke his shoulder. He was arrested shortly thereafter, and his imprisonment stalled the party's progress for months.

Seeking an End to Despair

From the end of the First World War through World War II, many people in Europe—and particularly those in Germany—showed a new interest in psychic powers, astrology, and spiritualism. Some Germans turned to seers and the séance table for the same reason they embraced the tyrant Adolf Hitler: for hope. The pain of their defeat in World War I, exacerbated by stringent peace terms and a hugely inflated economy, had left them with an oppressive sense of despair. They flocked to anyone who painted a bright picture of the future. The Nazis themselves, although they publicly scorned paranormal endeavors and eventually persecuted fortunetellers, nonetheless privately tolerated occult activity in their own ranks. They even ordered research in 1939 into psi phenomena and dowsing.

In the rest of Europe, psychics and astrologers found themselves deluged with clients, especially after World War II began. And British intelligence forces, sensing Nazi ambivalence toward the paranormal, launched an occult propaganda attack intended to misdirect Nazi officials and undermine German morale. The important roles played by psi, astrology, and occultism during Europe's bleakest years are examined on these pages.

The Prophet of the Third Reich

Between the wars, opportunists in Germany were quick to capitalize on popular interest in the paranormal—and to attach themselves to the increasingly powerful Nazis. Erik Jan Hanussen *(above, right)* did both.

Born Hermann Steinschneider, son of a Jewish itinerant performer, Hanussen learned at an early age to please a crowd. He claimed to possess psychic powers and soon styled himself as a clairvoyant. Changing his name to Erik Jan Hanussen—and boasting descent from Danish nobles—he joined the Nazi party in Berlin in 1931 and started a propagandist newspaper. He also set up what he called his Palace of the Occult—a flamboyant hall of magic where he staged dramatic séances sometimes attended by Nazi officials.

On one such occasion, Hanussen fell into a trance, then described a great hall that his audience recognized as the Reichstag, the lower house of the German parliament. According to the seer, flames were leaping from the building—flames set, he averred, by those jealous of Hitler's power.

The very next night, February 27, 1933, the Reichstag was torched *(above)*. Hitler's Communist opponents took the blame, although history has shown that a Dutch communist working alone was responsible. Hanussen's startlingly accurate prophecy was chalked up to his psychic prowess rather than to complicity, but less than a month later, Nazi storm troopers shot him dead: He had offended a Nazi leader by asking him to repay a debt.

Absorbed in his work and appearing almost demonic, Erik Jan Hanussen (left) gestures as he hypnotizes a client in 1930. Those who knew him said the clairvoyant possessed a mesmerizing power over people.

Hanussen records his prophecies on tape in his study in 1933 (right). The sculpture on the shelf above him was said to be a representation of Hanussen receiving psychic powers at the hands of a higher being.

Seated in the center of an eerily lit séance table (above), Hanussen holds his clients in thrall at his Palace of the Occult. It was during such a gathering that he predicted the Reichstag fire.

Salesmen hawk Hanussen's Berlin Weekly in this 1932 photograph (right). Subscribers received free psychic advice from Hanussen, dubbed the Prophet of the Third Reich.

Rewriting Nostradamus

In 1939, Nazi propaganda minister Joseph Goebbels hit on a clever tactic for psychological warfare: propaganda based on prophecies of the sixteenth-century French astrologer Nostradamus. Swiss prognosticator Karl Ernst Krafft was to carry out the plan.

Krafft had already proved himself a talented seer. On November 2, 1939, he had predicted mortal danger for Hitler between the seventh and tenth of the month. On November 8, Hitler spoke at a rally commemorating the anniversary of the Munich Beer Hall Putsch. Minutes after he had left the gathering, a bomb exploded behind the podium from which he had spoken.

Krafft was detained by Nazi police, but he convinced them he was a seer, not a murderer, and was soon as-signed to the Nostradamus project. He put a dubious pro-Nazi slant on many of the astrologer's vague predictions, in one case even construing a mention of the grand duke of Armenia to be a reference to Hitler. Krafft may also have fathered the later notion that Nostradamus had predicted the German blitzkrieg that resulted in the 1940 occupation of Paris (above).

Hitler pauses for applause during a speech at the Bürgerbräu beer cellar in Munich on November 8, 1939. Minutes after he left the building, a time bomb behind the swastika-emblazoned flag exploded, fulfilling Krafft's prophecy.

Krafft produced a facsimile edition (below) of the nearly 400-year-old predictions of Nostradamus (left). He also wrote interpretive pamphlets—such as the one lying atop the book—that often contained ardent Nazi propaganda.

Karl Ernst Krafft, pictured here as a teenager in 1916, later said that he experienced his first psychic vision at about this time; it was a premonition of his sister's death in 1919.

63

Mysticism in the Nazis' Inner Circle

Rumors of Hitler's reliance upon astrologers circulated for the duration of his rule. Although in hindsight it appears that the Führer did not regularly dabble in the occult, some of his subordinates did, and their interest in the subject subtly affected the history of the Third Reich.

Heinrich Himmler, chief of the Nazi protection squad (SS), is said to have consulted with an astrologer before making important decisions—and to have asked when might be an opportune time to supplant Hitler. But Himmler's grandest display of occult belief was in his police force. The SS was a true secret society, rife with all manner of mystical trappings, from arcane symbols to elaborate rituals.

Himmler restored a seventeenth-century fortress, Wewelsburg Castle *(above)*, to serve as the SS high temple. Smitten with Arthurian lore, he built a round table and a memorial hall for his "twelve knights"—his best men. He also built a sanctuary for the Holy Grail and sent a young scholar on an inconclusive quest for it in 1937.

Another high-ranking Nazi, Hitler's deputy Rudolf Hess, supposedly relied on the counsel of an amateur astrologer. In a desperate attempt to secure Hitler's favor, Hess planned a secret mission and allowed his occult adviser to select a fortuitous day. On May 10, 1941, Hess flew alone to Scotland, hoping to forge an accord between the Germans and their fellow Aryans in Great Britain. The mission failed miserably and cost Hess his career.

Himmler reviews Viennese police units during the Anschluss, the German-forced union with Austria in 1938. The SS leader is said to have bombarded his astrologer with questions concerning how and when Hitler's reign—and his life—would end.

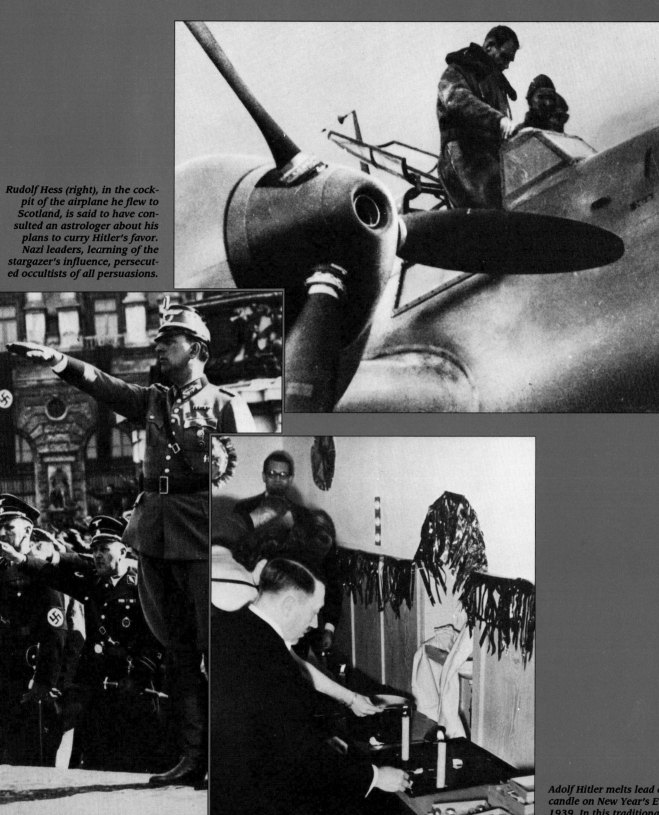

Rudolf Hess (right), in the cockpit of the airplane he flew to Scotland, is said to have consulted an astrologer about his plans to curry Hitler's favor. Nazi leaders, learning of the stargazer's influence, persecuted occultists of all persuasions.

Adolf Hitler melts lead over a candle on New Year's Eve in 1939. In this traditional German ritual, one reads the shape formed when the molten lead is dropped into water. Hitler opposed most occult practices but probably approved Himmler's successful use of clairvoyants, astrologers, and dowsers to locate abducted Italian dictator Benito Mussolini in 1943.

Psi in Troubled Poland

During the late 1930s, as Hitler's forces waited hungrily for the opportunity to pounce on neighboring Poland, two psychics in that country were becoming well known among their compatriots. One, Wolf Messing *(below)*, successfully foretold the failure of the German attack on Russia, and is also thought to have correctly predicted the circumstances of Hitler's death.

These bleak foreshadowings nearly cost Messing his life. After the German occupation of Poland, the Gestapo imprisoned the seer and sentenced him to death. Messing managed to escape, however, and later claimed that he had foiled his captors by exerting psychic control over them, compelling his guards to gather in his cell and stay there while he slipped away.

Another Polish psychic, Stefan Ossowiecki *(below, right)*, managed to elude capture even though he lived near a Gestapo office. Ossowiecki claimed to have seen auras in his youth and purportedly possessed gifts of clairvoyance and psychokinesis.

When the Germans bombed Warsaw in 1939, leaving parts of the city a skeletal ruin *(right)*, Ossowiecki chose to remain in order to help his fellow Poles. People reportedly lined up outside his apartment every day in 1940 and 1941 to inquire about vanished loved ones. In many cases, the psychic was able to mentally locate the missing persons; in some cases he led the inquirers to their loved ones' graves.

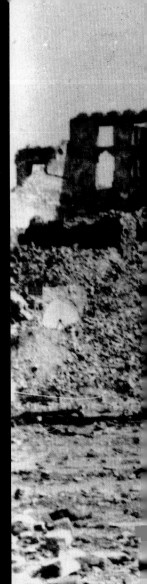

After his escape from a Gestapo prison, Wolf Messing—shown here in 1967—fled to the Soviet Union. There he told premier Joseph Stalin that Hitler, who was then a political ally, would become a dreaded enemy. The prophecy soon came to pass.

Stefan Ossowiecki relaxes with a book at his Warsaw home. The seer, who used his gift to soothe his fellow Poles, was killed in August 1944 in a Nazi massacre of Polish civilians.

Denis Sefton Delmer (below) broadcasts a spurious German radio show from a studio near London. Fluent in German from his early life in Berlin, Delmer masterminded the psychological warfare campaign that included occult propaganda.

An expatriate astrologer from Berlin, Louis de Wohl (right) wrote propaganda for Delmer. He crafted a book of bogus prophecies—which he attributed to the ever-popular Nostradamus—and provided stinging anti-German interpretations.

A Crafty British Plot

As the war raged on in 1941, the British launched a cunning campaign designed to erode enemy confidence. An element of this plan—which consisted largely of bogus German radio broadcasts and publications—was the use of slanted occult propaganda.

One broadcast, "Astrologie und Okkultismus," featured a German-speaking actress who claimed to receive messages from dead German soldiers that she then transmitted over the airwaves. The broadcast soon ceased, apparently because the actress was unable to refrain from chuckling while reading the scripts. With more success, the British Political Warfare Executive Office printed counterfeit German astrology magazines. Subtly written to confuse or dishearten the

German public, the prophecies were dated to past months so they would appear to predict current events.

At about the same time, British naval commander Ian Fleming—who later wrote the James Bond stories—purposefully leaked a false rumor to the Germans: The British, he revealed, were using pendulum-wielding psychics to dowse the location of enemy U-boats. This seemed plausible to the Germans because it coincided with an increase in British sinkings of submarines *(right)*. In truth, the sinkings resulted not from the input of psychics but from new technology and the fortuitous capture of a German decoding device. The unwitting Germans hired a dowser of their own in a vain attempt to answer the British triumphs.

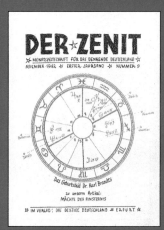

Ian Fleming, reflecting in his study in 1958, started the submarine-dowsing rumor that flummoxed German Intelligence. Fleming nurtured an interest in the occult, although he is said to have masked it with feigned cynicism.

Clever British propagandists faked an astrology magazine (above, left), using a name similar to that of a German publication (above, right). Despite its appearance, some Germans— including one admiral—followed the false journal's advice.

CHAPTER 2

The Psychic Cold War

he February 1960 issue of the popular French magazine *Science et Vie* informed its readers of an astounding communications breakthrough. In the summer of 1959, the magazine reported, the American nuclear-powered submarine USS *Nautilus* had been dispatched under the Arctic ice pack to a zone normally hidden from the most sensitive detectors of friend and foe alike. No technology then known could reliably breach the barriers of ice, water, and steel that cut a submerged polar vessel off from the rest of the world. Yet according to the article, written by one of the magazine's editors, Gérald Messadié, the hidden submarine had regularly received messages from a distant base—messages conveyed through the mind of a navy lieutenant in telepathic contact with a "sender" thousands of miles away.

A best-selling book, *Le Matin de Magicien* by journalists Jacques Bergier and Louis Pauwels, soon added more details to the *Nautilus* story. According to the book and the earlier article, the *Nautilus* project had begun on July 25, 1959, and continued for sixteen days. The designated sender, stationed at the Westinghouse laboratory in Friendship, Maryland, was identified only as Smith, a student at Duke University. The receiver aboard the *Nautilus* was referred to as Lieutenant Jones.

At two prearranged times each day, according to the French accounts, Smith stationed himself at a machine at Westinghouse that shuffled a thousand cards, each marked with either a square, a cross, a star, a circle, or wavy lines. The device dropped five cards—one at a time, at one-minute intervals—in front of Smith, who was directed to transmit his "visual impressions" of each successive card by concentrating on memorizing its appearance. He also drew a picture of the card's symbol on a piece of paper. After each test, Smith sealed his drawings in an envelope, which was then locked in a safe.

At the same time Smith was attempting to telepathically transmit the images on the cards one by one, Lieutenant Jones, aboard the *Nautilus,* was attempting to receive them in the same order. Recording his mental impressions, Jones drew a series of five symbols on a piece of paper. Then, after each test run, according to the French journalists, he sealed the results in an envelope. Jones then turned the envelope over to the submarine's skipper, Captain William Anderson, who locked it in his safe. For the duration of the study, Jones never left his stateroom; his only visitor was a sailor who brought his meals and took care of routine chores.

When the experiment ended, the *Nautilus* returned to its base at Groton, Connecticut, and—as the story went—the envelopes from Captain Anderson's safe were sped by car and plane to the Westinghouse laboratory. There the drawings by Smith and Jones were finally compared. When the results were tabulated, more than 70 percent of the drawings matched—a figure far in excess of the number, about 20 percent, to be expected from random chance. Separated from his telepathic partner by thousands of miles as well as a thick layer of ice, Jones had apparently received nearly three-quarters of the images transmitted by Smith.

Although the *Nautilus* incident was well reported in Europe, the story received little notice in the United States, perhaps because military officials vehemently denied it had ever happened. Air Force Colonel William Bowers, who had supposedly run the test, told an American reporter flatly that "the experiment in which I was alleged to have participated never took place." Captain Anderson, who was said to have kept the sealed envelopes in his cabin safe, was equally direct. Although his vessel had at times "engaged in a very wide variety of activities," he commented dryly, "certainly these did not include experiments in mental telepathy." He added that on

the day the *Nautilus* had allegedly begun receiving messages under the polar icecap the sub was actually out of the water, undergoing its first major overhaul in a Portsmouth, New Hampshire, dry dock.

In the years that followed, skeptics and psychic enthusiasts alike came to agree that the navy's denials were probably true. The *Nautilus* incident was apparently a hoax concocted by Jacques Bergier, a Russian-born journalist who lived in Paris. Bergier, who boasted of extensive contacts in the world of international espionage, was a wellspring of exotic military information for French publications. He had originally fed the *Nautilus* story to an unwitting Gérald Messadié, who wrote the *Science et Vie* article. Later, Bergier coauthored the book that offered more details. After Bergier's death in 1978, Messadié expressed regrets over his role in spreading what he had come to believe was a false story. The brilliant Bergier, Messadié said, had been utterly reliable most of the time, but was "sometimes prone to elaborations that verged on pranks, not to say hoaxes, and I don't believe I was then critical enough to judge such information."

In its day, however, the dubious story of the *Nautilus* psi experiment had a galvanizing effect on observers in Moscow, where the tale was widely believed. After all, Soviet military analysts hardly expected their American counterparts to confirm such obviously sensitive research. At the same time, eager Soviet parapsychologists seized upon the American "advance" as a justification for expanding their own work. During

subsequent years, one irony was heaped on another when the intensified Soviet psi effort—sparked by the supposed *Nautilus* experiment—created pressures on the American military to increase its own investment in parapsychological research. Whether or not he meant to, the mischievous Bergier had helped to instigate a decades-long psychic cold war, an escalating battle of the parapsychologists in which scientists and strategists on both sides sought to be the first to find military applications for such supposed extrasensory phenomena as telepathy, precognition, and clairvoyance.

In their research, West and East cast wide nets, finding uses for astrologers as well as psychics and looking into technologies that purportedly tapped natural psi energies to locate or destroy enemy installations and ships. In the rush to be the first nation to harness those energies for military purposes, neither the Americans nor the Soviets were above reaching into a bag of dirty tricks. On more than one occasion, one side or the other is thought to have mounted an elaborate disinformation campaign, making misleading disclosures intended to set their opponent off on a wasteful wild-goose chase. Some have speculated that the *Nautilus* affair itself was no playful hoax, but rather one of the earliest disinformation ploys. But even if Bergier planted the story, no one could confidently say for whom he was working. Some observers suggest the hoax originated with the Americans, to intimidate their Soviet foes, while others believe that Soviet parapsychologists might have fabricated the story to get more funding for their own research.

Whatever triggered the psychic cold war, the stakes of the struggle were high indeed. If psi powers proved to be real and controllable, they would have enormous impact on both open and covert conflicts. In theory, a well-trained agent with accurate extrasensory perception could penetrate enemy installations, read secret plans, and break communication codes. A field commander could anticipate an adversary's every action, gaining incalculable tactical advantage. Psi powers—if they existed—might also be aimed at enemy troops and leaders, inducing sickness, disorientation, or death from a distance.

In situations calling for more subtle action, a psi agent might seek to modify enemy behavior telepathically, by planting thoughts in the minds of individuals or by hypnotizing them. In theory, psi capabilities could also offer a

means of secret long-distance communication or could even provide psychic shields to conceal sensitive information or classified military installations.

Long before the twentieth-century cold war, military and political leaders sought practical uses for the strange powers some believe the human mind possesses. One of the earliest accounts of psychic spying appears in the Old Testament. According to the Second Book of Kings, the prophet Elisha warned Israel's government of Syrian troop movements, which he saw not with his eyes, he said, but in his mind. The Bible recounts that Elisha's visions spared Israel from military defeat several times, while the Syrian king was so perplexed by his enemy's foreknowledge that he questioned his own people, angrily searching for a traitor.

Attempts at cultivating paranormal powers for use in combat were also widespread in the ancient world. In *The Art of War,* a treatise written in 500 BC, the Chinese general Sun Tzu cited the importance of a force called *qi,* a kind of vital energy, for success in battle. A superior warrior, Sun Tzu taught that by controlling the flow of qi through the body one could use it to influence adversaries. Supplementing conventional tactics with skilled management of qi, a leader could introduce illusions and weakness in the minds of the enemy. A foot soldier trained in the ways of qi could achieve a deadly calm even in the chaos of combat. Such a fighter was said to be able to wrest insuperable advantage from even a slight break in an enemy's concentration.

Many rulers of medieval and Renaissance Europe, also seeking an advantage over those who would challenge them, had psychics and seers at their beck and call. Among the most renowned was John Dee, an early scientist who served as court astrologer for Queen Elizabeth I of England. An experimenter in many occult activities, Dee used a crystal ball, which he called the "shew stone," to receive messages from an assemblage of spirits known as "the nine." One extraordinary story, probably apocryphal, has it that the stone informed Dee of a plot by Spanish agents to burn the forests that provided raw material for the English fleet. If the plot was indeed real, Dee's discovery may have changed history. Without its forests, England would have been hard pressed to mount an effective opposition to the Spanish Armada in 1588.

European interest in psychic spying continued, intensifying centuries later during and immediately following the turmoil of World War I. According to an article by Czechoslovakian officer Karel Hejbalik, published in 1925 under the title "Clairvoyance, Hypnotism, and Magnetic Healing at the Service of the Military," dowsers employed during the war by the Czech army to find drinking water had also succeeded in pinpointing traps and land mines. Furthermore, Hejbalik wrote, during a campaign against Hungary in 1919 he had hypnotized two soldiers under his command, heightening their psi abilities so they could observe enemy

According to the Greek historian Herodotus, King Croesus of Lydia (above) once asked the famed oracle at Delphi whether to go to war with Persia. After inhaling sacred fumes, the priestess told him such a war would "overthrow the strength of an empire." Taking this as a sign of encouragement, Croesus attacked, only to be defeated and captured. The oracle had been right, according to Herodotus—but it was Lydia, not Persia, that was destined to fall.

dispositions telepathically. Hejbalik maintained that the information that had been gained through psi channels proved to be accurate whenever it could be checked by independent means, a claim confirmed by Zdeněk Rejdák, a Czech psi researcher who interviewed some of the subjects of the experiments.

The involvement of psychics in modern warfare reached new heights with World War II, as many of the contending powers engaged sensitives for research, espionage, and a variety of other operations *(pages 58-69).* The United States Navy was a leader in funding various experiments—generally unsuccessful—that sought psychic solutions to problems encountered in the new global war. One study is said to have tried in vain to discover a psychic navigation system in homing pigeons, in the hope of finding new ways of navigating submerged submarines and night bombers. Despite the failure of the navy's wartime studies, journalists who follow psi warfare contend that the navy continued its funding of psychic research well beyond the war years, with a particular emphasis on submarines.

Nor was the navy the only branch of the armed forces to explore psi powers in peacetime. In 1952, the U.S. Army decided to find out whether dogs could be taught to use clairvoyance to find land mines, the hair-trigger buried explosives that claim many lives on the battlefield. Research into this notion was duly undertaken by Joseph Rhine, a

Napoleon Bonaparte, striking a heroic pose in this 1810 portrait, allegedly used astrology and numerology to assess his senior officers.

well-known psychologist from Duke University's Parapsychology Laboratory, who was among the first to pursue the scientific study of psi phenomena in the United States.

According to an article Rhine published on the topic years later, he carried out a series of experiments on an isolated beach near San Francisco, using two German shepherds named Tessie and Binnie. Both dogs had been trained to sit as an indication of finding a dummy land mine, a small wooden box planted under the sand. Before each test run, a research team buried several boxes along so-called target lines fifteen to twenty-five yards long. To remove all sensory clues to the locations of the boxes, each target line was covered in six to twelve inches of water.

To perform a test, one of the two dogs and its handler—both totally isolated during the placement of the "mines"—walked along the target line. Every place at which the dog sat down was then marked by the handler with a thin white stake. Another researcher, who also did not know where the dummy mines were located, recorded the position of each stake.

On three consecutive June days, Tessie and Binnie patiently went through twenty-four tests apiece on the windy beach. Random chance would have produced a success rate of 20 percent, according to Rhine; the dogs' success rate was 37.5 percent, almost twice as high. In subsequent tests in July and August, they did even better, with a 44.2 percent success rate. In later tests, however, the number of "hits"—that is, the number of times the dogs successfully located a buried dummy mine—began to fall off. Nevertheless, the overall success rate achieved in the experiments remained significantly better than chance.

Despite this impressive performance by the two dogs, the army abandoned the project at the testing stage. A 40-percent success rate was far better than that expected from

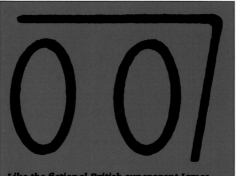

Like the fictional British superagent James Bond, Elizabethan seer and spy John Dee went by the code name 007, written in the peculiar way shown above. The two zeros, according to Dee, symbolize human eyes; the seven is the sum of the two eyes, the four other senses, and the mystical acquisition of knowledge.

chance alone, but it would do little to prevent casualties in a real minefield. Furthermore, the dogs were unable to search out the mines independently. They required handlers who, with the dogs, would be at substantial risk.

While the army was testing canine psychic powers on the beach, the Central Intelligence Agency (CIA) was reportedly monitoring psi research around the world. According to some writers on psychic warfare, the CIA also undertook a variety of secret studies—with code names such as Bluebird, Artichoke, and MK-ULTRA—aimed at developing reliable psychic abilities in experimental subjects.

Meanwhile, as explained in the memoirs of former CIA agent Miles Copeland, another branch of the agency had already found its own use for the occult—albeit a fraudulent one. In the early 1950s, Robert Mandlestam, an inventive young member of the agency's political action unit, persuaded his superiors to attempt to influence the actions of certain foreign leaders by planting American-controlled astrologers in their circles of advisers.

As Copeland told the story in his 1989 book *The Game Player*, the astrology scheme took more than a decade to bear fruit. Its first success came in 1966, when Kwame Nkrumah, president of Ghana, consulted his CIA-trained seer about an invitation to visit China. The astrologer assured the increasingly unpopular Nkrumah that the stars were auspicious for such a trip, and Nkrumah made the fateful decision to leave Ghana for some weeks. While he was out of the country, a coup brought to power Lieutenant General Joseph A. Ankrah, a leader favored by the United States. The program reaped still more success a few months later, according to Copeland, when information from a computerized astrology program developed by the CIA convinced President Achmed Sukarno of Indonesia that he should undertake several un-

Uncanny Mountain Men

As United States soldiers battled American Indians for control of western lands, the cavalry's chances of victory—or simple survival—depended in large part on the seasoned scouts who guided them through unfamiliar hostile terrain. Knowledgeable in Indian ways, such "mountain men" were also expert trackers, able to detect the presence of hostile forces from hints as subtle as the movement of a distant bighorn sheep. Many of their comrades also credited the scouts with a true sixth sense—an intuitive, perhaps psychic, faculty that warned them of impending danger. Some scouts agreed; others, such as James Butler "Wild Bill" Hickok, claimed mysterious spirit forces protected them; still others experienced premonitions they said warned of danger or sudden death.

According to at least one source, cavalry commanders ignored such psychic warnings at their peril. In 1865, General Patrick Connor led a campaign into the Powder River region of Montana Territory to put down Indian incursions into white settlements. One night, chief scout Jim Bridger *(right)* heard the eerie howl of a spirit called the Medicine Wolf, a sign of impending danger. Bridger wanted to move camp; Connor contemptuously refused—a decision he may have come to regret. In the days that followed, supply shortages, military failures, and bitter winter storms dogged the ill-fated expedition—and eventually cost him his command.

specified actions that jibed nicely with United States policy.

While the CIA took advantage of the paranormal beliefs of some world leaders, the United States military began testing psi powers in a shooting war. The United States Marine Corps, deeply embroiled in the Vietnam conflict by 1966, was frustrated by the difficulty of locating supply caches and finding the tunnels used by the Vietcong to hide men and materials throughout the country. A new approach to the job arose from a suggestion by Louis Matacia, a Virginia land surveyor who worked as a consultant for the marines. Matacia had enjoyed considerable success as a professional dowser, searching out underground utility lines with no more than a pair of L-shaped wires cut from coat hangers. The same technique, he told the marines, ought to work for Vietcong tunnels.

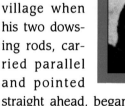

ost of the officers who heard Matacia's suggestion reacted skeptically. But one officer, a Major T. F. Manley, was apparently more open-minded. To try out the dowsing idea, Manley arranged a full-scale test at a mock Vietnamese village located at the Marine Corps base in Quantico, Virginia. The village was used to provide tactical training to Vietnam-bound marines. It featured authentic thatched huts, rice paddies, and pigpens—as well as a network of tunnels and a fearsome array of booby traps.

According to an account of the test provided by paranormal investigator Christopher Bird in his 1979 book *The Divining Hand,* the soft-spoken Matacia had just entered the village when his two dowsing rods, carried parallel and pointed straight ahead, began to separate, swinging outward toward huts on either side of him. "Well, now, that's got to be a tunnel of some kind," Matacia drawled. As the marine observers laid a white ribbon between the huts to record the finding, Matacia went on to note that the tunnel sloped from one house to the other. A captain who descended into the tunnel network discovered a foot of water standing at the end of the tunnel Matacia had said was deeper.

As Matacia walked through the village, his dowsing rods (the marines called them "wire rudders") indicated tunnels, hidden rooms, underground pipes and wires, and even a false wall hiding a small room that could conceal several guerrilla fighters. Matacia completed his tour of the village in less than half an hour, reportedly revealing most of the subterranean maze with no erroneous calls. His escorts were so excited by the results that some immediately tried their hands with the "rudders"—and had unexpected success. Matacia later told the marines that the only people he considered unlikely to master the art of dowsing were the mentally ill, the mentally retarded, and the unshakably skeptical.

By March 1967, *The Observer,* a newspaper published for United States troops in Vietnam, reported that Matacia's dowsing rods had been introduced to marines in the field.

Skillfully camouflaged entrances lead to a labyrinth of narrow tunnels, wells, and bunkers in this subterranean Vietcong complex discovered in 1965. In its often fruitless search to locate such underground hiding places, the Marine Corps tried training soldiers like the one at left to use wire dowsing rods.

1. **AIR VENTS**
2. **NOTCHED DIRT STEPS**
3. **WATER**
4. **CAMOUFLAGED COVER**
5. **CAMOUFLAGED VENT HOLE**
6. **NORMAL WELL TOP**
7. **CAMOUFLAGED ENTRANCE COVERS**

50-100M

Although at first the combat troops were as dubious as their counterparts in Virginia had been, the wire rudders did locate "a few" Vietcong tunnels, according to published accounts. After five months, however, the plan was withdrawn. The Quantico Training and Development Command had concluded that dowsing required "special skills that cannot be taught to the average marine."

Even before the marines laid down their divining rods, research on military uses of psi powers had begun to boom in the Soviet Union—in large part because of European reports of the supposed psi experiment aboard the *Nautilus* submarine. Publicity on the subject in the early 1960s had spurred the Kremlin to authorize more psychic research, a field of study that had fallen into official disrepute in the 1940s. At that time, the official Soviet encyclopedia disparaged telepathy as an "anti-social, idealist fiction about man's supernatural power," a belief anathema to the materialistic Soviet state. Government pressure had also put an end to pioneering psi research by Soviet physiologist Leonid Vasiliev at the Leningrad Institute for Brain Research. Now Vasiliev saw the reported *Nautilus* study as a "totally unex-

pected foreign confirmation" of his earlier work and urged that those studies be resumed.

By 1962 Vasiliev had regained at least tacit official support, publishing a book called *Experiments in Distant Influence.* He wrote that the Americans had improved on his own research—which had involved one subject putting another to sleep at a distance—by showing that telepathic influences "spanned longer distances and overcame greater physical obstacles," including deep water and the sealed metal hull of a submarine.

Vasiliev went on to spend much of the 1960s studying the abilities of an enigmatic Soviet psychic named Nina Kulagina. First drawn by Kulagina's reputation for convincing demonstrations of psychic ability, Vasiliev was most interested in her telekinetic talents, which reportedly included the ability to move a compass needle with mind power alone. Other observers were less impressed. During this period Soviet newspapers routinely attacked Kulagina as a fraud, attributing her powers to magnets concealed in "intimate places" about her body. Western researchers who sought to test Kulagina found she had a variety of reasons that kept her from being available for rigorous observation.

The purported *Nautilus* results inspired other Soviet parapsychology initiatives as well. Although psi research remained controversial among Soviet scientists, in many ways it fit neatly into prevailing Soviet theories of psychology, which offered a materialistic view of the human mind as merely an elaborate biological apparatus with complex electrochemical processes that allowed it to receive information and induce energies. Soviet experiments in parapsychology were aimed at tuning up these physical processes, making the brain more sensitive, powerful, and open to outside influences.

One leading proponent of this view was Vasiliev's colleague Bernard Kazhinsky, author of a 1962 book entitled *Biological Radio Communications*. The work describes Kazhinsky's theory about telepathy: He believed mental information could be conveyed over long distances by the same kind of electromagnetic waves used in radio transmissions. The human brain and nervous system, he wrote, "is a repository of highly sophisticated instruments of biological radio communication," capable of transmitting sensations and experiences with a tiny fraction of the energy used to power a conventional radio transmitter. The implications for military communications were potentially wide ranging.

Advancing under the banner unfurled by Vasiliev and Kazhinsky, a new generation of Soviet parapsychologists eagerly pursued the study of psychic powers, generally with a view to possible military applications. As the official attitude toward their work softened, they found their way to international parapsychology conferences, where they peppered Western colleagues with questions about their research and occasionally lifted the shroud of secrecy that ordinarily hid the most interesting work in the Soviet Union. One frequent Soviet player was Eduard Naumov, a gregarious researcher who maintained extensive contacts with the West throughout the 1960s.

In 1968, after providing several seemingly indiscreet revelations at a Moscow parapsychology conference he had helped organize, Naumov found himself the focus of attention. At the meeting, which attracted a number of Western parapsychological researchers eager to pick up clues about the direction of secret Soviet research, Naumov revealed that a Soviet naval intelligence operation had successfully imitated the supposed *Nautilus* experiment. The Soviet research had succeeded, he said, in achieving a telepathic connection between a submerged submarine and a shore station. Naumov also claimed that in a separate experiment a military intelligence unit had developed a method for intercepting and monitoring telepathic exchanges between two people—a sort of psychic wiretap.

Given that the *Nautilus* experiment was by then considered a hoax, many Western observers were skeptical of Naumov's hints. An evaluation of his claims was complicated by the fact that during the Moscow conference the Soviet press had routinely condemned all parapsychological research as irrelevant and decadent.

Despite such official Soviet ambivalence, news of psychic experiments filtering out of the Soviet Union had by this time fueled fears in the West that a "psychic gap" was opening. A few popular books and articles painted doomsday scenarios of psychic Soviet troops massing for an eventual attack. Among American defense analysts of a less apocalyptic bent, responses to the supposed Soviet lead in psychic warfare varied from complete disbelief to acute dismay. Some, perhaps most, were convinced that reports of Soviet experiments were nothing more than artful disinformation, intended to make the United States waste money in a one-sided psychic arms race. Others suggested that the disinformation might be coming from researchers on their own side, eager to drum up funding for American investigation into similar topics.

In a classified 1972 report later released by the CIA, that agency attempted a reasoned analysis of the threat of Soviet psychic warfare. Perhaps uncertain of its footing in this field, the CIA produced a document containing a mixture of hedging and alarmism. "Soviet efforts in the field of psi research, sooner or later, might enable them to do some of the following," analysts wrote. "(a) Know the contents of top secret U.S. documents, the movements of our troops and ships and the location and nature of our military installations. (b) Mould the thoughts of key U.S. military and civilian leaders at a distance. (c) Cause the instant death of any U.S. official at a distance. (d) Disable, at a distance, U.S.

eye on the field, watching for technologies with possible intelligence or military uses. One of the earliest results of this survey came in 1973, when the agency happened upon a promising investigation of clairvoyance—the ability to see objects or actions at a seemingly impossible distance in space or time—being conducted at the Stanford Research Institute (later renamed SRI International) in Menlo Park, California, near San Francisco.

military equipment of all types including spacecraft.''

Although the report was at best highly speculative, a few within the military establishment and Congress eventually responded to its nebulous warning. During the late 1970s, North Carolina congressman Charles Rose assembled a small group of Capitol Hill colleagues who were interested in strategic American uses of parapsychology. Rose was well respected among his peers. He was a devout Presbyterian and former county prosecutor in North Carolina who had made himself the acknowledged computer expert of the House of Representatives, and he was a leading member of the House Select Committee on Intelligence.

On the subject of parapsychology, Rose thought that research into military applications of psi was hampered by skeptics within the Pentagon and the CIA. The congressman himself was far from skeptical. According to Ron McRae, a journalist who has worked with columnist Jack Anderson, Rose once tested telepathic influence by trying to get Thomas P. ''Tip'' O'Neill, then Speaker of the House of Representatives, to favor a project that would benefit Rose's district. (Since Rose refused to discuss the matter with McRae, the results of his political experiment are unknown.)

Meanwhile, in the wake of its own report, the CIA had already stepped up intelligence monitoring of most parapsychological research in the United States. By one account, half a dozen case officers were assigned to keep an

SRI was known as a source of serious, conservative science, and two reputable physicists were conducting the research. Harold Puthoff was well known as the inventor of a tunable infrared laser and as the author of *Fundamentals of Quantum Electronics,* a standard text in the field. His partner Russell Targ had done respected work with gas lasers.

Harold Puthoff had come to psychic research in the late 1960s through advanced particle physics. Speculating on the nature of certain hypothetical particles that theorists suggested could move backward and forward in time, Puthoff concluded that ''some of their properties were similar to the kinds of things that were reported for the psychic function." In 1972 he left his academic position at Stanford University to join SRI, where he received permission to conduct full-time psi research. He was joined by Targ, whose own longstanding interest in psychic research had led him to invent an electronic device that he used to conduct ESP experiments in his spare time, including tests of his young daughter's psi abilities.

Responsible for raising their own funds, the SRI researchers got their first grant from the Science Unlimited Research Foundation (SURF), an organization founded by George W. Church, a Texas entrepreneur who owned a fried-chicken restaurant franchise. Soon Targ embarked on a quest for government funding. To avoid supernatural connotations, he presented the idea of clairvoyance as "remote viewing." These efforts paid off when Puthoff and Targ reached an agreement with the CIA—and possibly other government agencies—to further study remote viewing.

Under the CIA plan, a group at the intelligence agency would select a pool of specific locations around the globe, including secret sites in the United States, the Soviet Union, and China. After other CIA officers picked sites at random from the pool, the latitude and longitude of each location would be transmitted in code to SRI. There, participants would be asked to describe what they could "see" at the place indicated by those coordinates. This gave the project its name: SCANATE, for SCANning by coordinATE.

To eliminate any chance of cheating, some of the sites in the Soviet Union and China were deliberately chosen from territory then unknown to the CIA. These areas were scheduled for observation by spy satellites two or three months after the remote-viewing tests. Until then, no one could say with certainty what was there.

Testing on the SCANATE project began in May 1973 and lasted two years. Most of the subjects had no significant psychic experience. Hella Hammid, who proved to be an accurate remote viewer, was a freelance photographer; Richard Bach was the author of the 1970 bestseller *Jonathan Livingston Seagull;* three other volunteers were SRI scientists and staff members. Two experienced subjects rounded out the SCANATE roster. One was professional psychic and artist Ingo Swann. The other was Pat Price, a businessman and retired police commissioner from Burbank, California. In volunteering his services to Puthoff over the telephone, Price recalled using his psychic abilities to find suspected criminals. On an impulse, Puthoff decided to put his caller to the test. He gave Price a set of coordinates from the experimental pool supplied by the CIA. Neither Puthoff nor Price knew it, but the coordinates were those of a military installation about 135 miles southwest of Washington, D.C.

Within days Puthoff received Price's response by mail. The five-page letter minutely described a complex of buildings and subterranean storage areas. The description began with a view from 1,500 feet above the site, then got closer and closer until Price recounted such details as the appearance of computer terminals and nameplates on desks. The

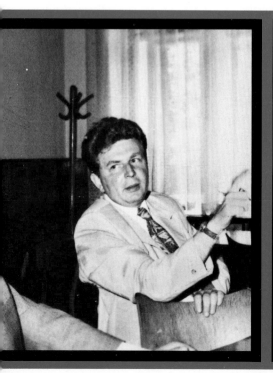

high point of the mental tour came when Price "mashed his head" into a locked file cabinet. The file folders inside, he reported, bore a curious set of labels: Cue Ball, Four Ball, Eight Ball, Fourteen Ball, Rackup, Side Pocket.

A somewhat bemused Puthoff passed along Price's description to his CIA contacts. To his surprise, they confirmed that Price's report was essentially correct. Furthermore, Puthoff's CIA handlers were certain that Price could not have come by his information through any normal channels. Price had apparently passed the informal screening test with flying colors.

Years later, however, some doubt would be cast on this particular SCANATE story. In 1977, science journalist John Wilhelm checked up on the coordinates in question and found only a pasture—"a sparse hillside, a few flocks of sheep, and lots of droppings." The matter became even more confusing when Wilhelm asked James Foote, a navy liaison to the SCANATE project, for an explanation. Foote checked with intelligence sources and reported that despite Wilhelm's findings, "it was a valid test as far as the investigators are concerned." Foote offered several theories, ranging from some error in specifying the coordinates to the idea that Price read the mind of one of SCANATE's military contacts rather than tuning in to the coordinates.

The truth of that initial test may never be known. But according to a number of articles and popular books about the project, including Ron McRae's 1984 work *Mind Wars,* SCANATE is said by most observers to have scored a number of impressive successes. Perhaps because of the project's semisecret status, the SCANATE results are usually presented anecdotally, however, with no summary statistics on the total number of hits and misses.

Some of the project's most striking results were achieved by Ingo Swann. In one case, the experimenters named the coordinates 49°20′ south, 70°14′ east and asked Swann to respond immediately without looking at a map. Swann described "an island, maybe a mountain sticking up through cloud cover. Terrain seems rocky. Very cold. I see some buildings rather mathematically laid out. One of them is orange. Two white cylindrical tanks, quite large." As Swann continued, he accurately described a French-Soviet weather research station on Kerguelen Island near the Antarctic Circle. He even got the station's outhouse right.

By the mid-1970s, the CIA pronounced its satisfaction with the SRI results, and an independent evaluation by defense analyst Joseph A. Ball reached a similar conclusion. But the future of military remote viewing remained uncertain. Although Ball agreed that the SRI study "produced manifestations of extrasensory perception sufficiently sharp and clear-cut to justify serious considerations of possible applications," he believed that remote viewing would never replace conventional methods. Psychic spying could supplement normal intelligence gathering, Ball wrote, but psi methods could never stand alone, because they were "capricious and unreliable."

SCANATE was only the beginning of remote-viewing research at SRI. Most of the SCANATE subjects also participated in more widely publicized experiments conducted throughout the 1970s for the navy and other government agencies. For these tests, a team of researchers visited a nearby site unknown to a viewer who remained at SRI. At an agreed-upon time, the viewer attempted to describe the team's surroundings and draw a picture of the site.

These experiments sometimes matched the success rates claimed for the initial SCANATE tests. Although no subjects had perfect scores, independent judges matched their descriptions and drawings with the correct targets at a rate far higher than would occur by chance. Pat Price was sometimes able to describe buildings, docks, roads, and gardens with great accuracy. In one case, he even recognized and named the target—the Hoover Tower on the nearby Stanford campus.

In 1977, SRI researchers conducted tests aboard a small submarine—bringing the psychic arms race full circle from the apocryphal *Nautilus* experiments. In two tests, the submersible *Taurus,* carrying a remote viewer as part of its five-person crew, was towed out to sea for miles before diving. Russell Targ wryly noted that one consequence of the long, choppy rides was that the subjects were probably the first psychics to demonstrate their abilities while seasick.

The *Taurus* then submerged near Santa Catalina Island, off the coast of southern California. The target sites for this study were six locations in the San Francisco Bay area, about 500 miles from the submarine. At a prearranged time two SRI researchers chose one of the targets by a random selection method, and visited it for fifteen minutes.

In the first experiment, which involved remote viewer Hella Hammid, the *Taurus* dove to a depth of more than 500 feet. At the assigned time, Hammid described that day's target as "a very tall looming object. A very, very huge, tall tree and a lot of space behind them. There almost feels like there is a dropoff or a palisade or a cliff behind them." The description seemed to fit the site, a hilltop in the Portola Valley, dominated by a large oak tree surrounded by smaller trees and underbrush.

For the second test, conducted with Ingo Swann, the *Taurus* submerged under 250 feet of seawater. Swann made a rough drawing of the impressions he received and provided a description of the target area: "Flat stone flooring, walls, small pool, reddish stone walk, large doors, walking around, an enclosed space." The judges considered that rather sketchy description a good match for the target, a shopping mall in Mountain View.

Although such apparent successes were common, the viewers often went wrong when they tried to interpret their impressions. In one early trial, Richard Bach accurately described the interior of a church visited by the target team, but he interpreted the altar as an airline check-in counter. This initial error gave rise to others; the cross behind the altar became, for Bach, the airline's logo displayed on the wall of the terminal. To avoid such problems, subjects were encouraged to describe only objects, settings, and actions.

A more positive finding came from a series of long-distance experiments, conducted cross-country, that showed roughly the same accuracy as the earlier Menlo Park tests. Distance evidently had little effect on remote-viewing ability—a hopeful sign for SRI's partners in the military and intelligence communities.

The SRI experiments also yielded a finding of potentially greater importance, one that Puthoff and Targ found so hard to believe that they nearly omitted it from their published report. In a section titled "Considerations Concerning Time," the two physicists recounted a few occasions in the laboratory when remote-viewing subjects spontaneously described target sites before the target teams arrived there —in fact, before the target had been chosen. Two of these reports were so accurate that the researchers felt compelled to study the effect further.

In subsequent tests described by Puthoff and Targ in a professional journal in 1976, the SRI team followed procedures identical to those for the remote-viewing experiments—except that each subject was asked to describe the target site during a fifteen-minute period that ended five minutes before the target was chosen, and twenty minutes before the researchers were due to arrive there. In four separate trials, Puthoff and Targ reported, their subjects scored four hits: a marina, a fountain in a formal garden, a swing set in a small park, and the Palo Alto City Hall. The researchers could offer no explanation for the unprecedented success of the experiments, which seemed to reveal the subjects' precognitive powers, nor for the exceptional accuracy of the transcribed descriptions.

These experiments marked the high point of Targ and Puthoff's collaboration. In 1982 Targ left the firm, citing dissatisfaction with the extent of military sponsorship of his work. He founded a psychic consulting firm called Delphi Associates, which reportedly made and lost a small fortune trading in silver futures. Puthoff left SRI a few years later.

While the CIA appeared satisfied with the results at SRI, the remote-viewing tests performed there had their share of critics. Some observers suggested that the judging procedure, which involved matching fragmented descriptions to known target sites, allowed too much room for interpretation. Furthermore, because the subjects were often taken to a site they had "viewed" and then tested on that same site again, subsequent target descriptions could be colored in ways that influenced the judging.

A more controversial criticism of the tests came from observers who pointed out that Swann, Price, and several SRI staff members, including Puthoff, were associated with the Church of Scientology, an organization that endorses the existence of telepathy and out-of-body travel. Most accounts of the SRI project agree that Puthoff, Swann, and Price did, at a minimum, take various Scientology courses at different times. For his part, science reporter John Wilhelm asserts unequivocally that all three are Operational Thetans—the highest rank in the church. Some critics suggested that a desire to prove their church right could have biased the researchers, consciously or unconsciously.

Puthoff himself answered that incendiary suggestion by pointing to the elaborate controls on the research. "When we carry on an experiment," he explained, "a major piece of the experiment is under control by people who don't have anything to do with Scientology." Non-Scientologist Russell Targ was less measured in his response, describing the entire issue as outright religious bigotry on the part of the critics. Logically, as Wilhelm himself acknowledges, the concentration of Scientologists at SRI could be explained by their natural interest in working on a subject in which they believed.

Midway through the 1970s, as American military investigation into psychic abilities continued at SRI and elsewhere, the official Soviet attitude toward psi research began to harden. One of the first to be affected was researcher Eduard Naumov. In 1974, after years of attacking Naumov in the press, Soviet authorities imprisoned him for "financial irregularities." The Associated Press reported that the psi investigator's real crime may have been a refusal to break off his contacts with Western researchers.

Although Naumov was released the following year, his incarceration marked a definite end to Soviet openness on psi-war research. From then on, Western researchers found their Soviet counterparts far more reluctant than in the past to discuss any psychic studies that might have military or intelligence uses. For many observers, this was simply further proof that the Soviets had psi secrets to hide.

That suspicion was strengthened in 1977 by an incident tangentially involving Eduard Naumov. After his release from prison in 1975, Naumov had found a temporary job at the Laboratory of Biophysics at the State Control Institute of Medical Biological Preparations in Moscow. Despite its name, the lab conducted a certain amount of psi research. In 1977, the man for whom Naumov had worked at the institute, Valery G. Petukhov, ran into even more trouble with the law than had Naumov. Petukhov was arrested by the KGB as he passed a scientific document, apparently an article on possible biological mechanisms of telepathy, to Robert Toth, the Moscow correspondent for the *Los Angeles Times.* Toth had a chance only to glance at the first page of the document before he was also detained. During his subsequent interrogation, it became clear to Toth that Soviet authorities believed that the document contained classified information of some importance. Some Western psi researchers, however, speculated that the incident was only another Soviet disinformation effort.

During the same period, American military efforts to keep up with the increasingly secretive Soviet research into psi had begun to veer from one eccentric endeavor to another. In the same year that Petukhov attempted to share his telepathy research with the West, the United States Navy spent $5,111 to buy a supposedly psychically powered device called a "multispectral image analyzer station." The instrument was the property of Charles Whitehouse, a Virginia chiropractor and psychic who marketed alleged psychotronic equipment—devices, often electronic, that are said to harness psi powers. Offering little explanation of the workings of his psychotronic tool, Whitehouse touted the little black box as a solution to the navy's antisubmarine problems, and assured his naval contacts that anyone who

Remote Viewing in the Laboratory

Ingo Swann was bored. The New York artist and psychic was closeted in 1973 with psi researcher Harold Puthoff at the Stanford Research Institute (SRI), a San Francisco think tank, trying to determine whether a red or a green laser was burning in the next room. Swann thought such tests trivialized his gifts. "Why don't we do something exciting?" he asked.

Swann was an old hand at remote-viewing tests, designed to measure clairvoyant abilities. The year before, Swann had taken part in experiments at the American Society for Psychical Research in which he was challenged to describe pictures and other objects that researchers had hidden out of view. Swann believed the results were significant because they demonstrated his ability to leave his physical body and float to where the objects lay. Now he wanted to replicate the trials, but at longer distances. Provided with only a latitude and longitude reading, Swann told Puthoff, he could view any location on the face of the earth.

Intrigued, Puthoff and fellow SRI researcher Russell Targ gave Swann the coordinates of a site lying to the northeast of Mount Hekla, a volcano on the island of Iceland. Without consulting a map, Swann instantly said, "Volcano to southwest. I think I am over ocean."

Suspecting that Swann's answer showed not so much psychic ability as a well-practiced familiarity with world geography, the researchers devised a series of stiffer tests involving more obscure coordinates. Swann performed just as well in describing these unfamiliar sites, including a little-known meteorological station on Kerguelen, a 2,000-square-mile island in the southern Indian Ocean.

In another trial, the psychic correctly answered "ocean" when he was given the coordinates of a site in the North Pacific. And after being supplied with the latitude and longitude of the eastern shore of Lake Victoria, in central Africa, Swann related an eerie sense of speeding over water and touching down on high ground to the west of a lake.

Swann's apparent success in such remote-viewing tests attracted considerable attention, including that of the Central Intelligence Agency, which hired SRI to investigate the remote-viewing phenomenon from 1973 to 1975. It also prompted Puthoff and Targ to expand the scope of their research to include a slightly different protocol: One or more so-called outbound experimenters, or beacons, visited nearby target sites while a viewer, kept in seclusion back at SRI, recorded his or her impressions of the beacons' locations. Independent judges then visited the sites to evaluate the accuracy of the viewer's descriptions.

The SRI team conducted more than fifty trials this way, about two-thirds of which were later considered matches. Others have reported similar successes in their attempts to replicate the SRI experiments. Examples of work from the Princeton Engineering Anomalies Research lab, the Mind Science Foundation in San Antonio, Texas, and the Mobius Society of Los Angeles appear on the following pages.

Psychic Ingo Swann, at home in Manhattan, reads an astrological chart before a painting he created in 1984. Swann has since given up painting to concentrate on psychic endeavors and writing.

You Can See Forever

In 1976, Puthoff and Targ turned their attention to a notion advanced by Soviet psi researchers that all psychic information was carried by extremely low frequency (ELF) electromagnetic radiation. Knowing that ELF waves grow weaker the farther they travel from their source, the SRI team surmised that remote viewers would have more difficulty describing distant targets than those nearby. The researchers devised a series of trials to test their hypothesis.

In one test, Susan Harris, a medical student at Tulane University in New Orleans, was asked to describe the whereabouts of two coexperimenters who visited a randomly selected location in California. Despite the great distance, Harris apparently was able to describe not only the target, a bank building, but also what the beacons were doing: During the viewing session, she drew a picture showing two stick figures playing catch with a Frisbee. According to Targ, at that moment Harris's colleagues were tossing an airplane that they had fashioned from a piece of scrap paper found at the site. Other SRI trials, such as the one shown here, also discredited the ELF theory.

A sunbathed concrete runway dominates both this photograph, taken by SRI researcher Harold Puthoff on the tiny Caribbean island of San Andrés on April 12, 1973, and the drawing above, sketched on the same day by a remote viewer in California.

Rome Calling Detroit

In November 1979, psi researchers Elmar Gruber and Marilyn Schlitz attempted to replicate the work of Puthoff and Targ—at an even greater distance. Each day for ten days, Gruber spent fifteen minutes at a randomly selected site in Rome, Italy; Schlitz, at her home in Detroit, wrote down her impressions of Gruber's location. The outcome impressed five judges who evaluated her descriptions: Despite odds of more than 100,000 to one, six of the ten trials were considered direct hits.

Targets varied from the roof of Saint Peter's Cathedral to the Villa Borghese.

On the sixth day, Gruber stood on a small hill overlooking the Rome International Airport *(below).* From there, he could see the runways, terminals, and planes as well as a nearby area where treasure seekers had dug countless small holes in hopes of unearthing ancient coins.

Schlitz began that day's remote-viewing session by drawing the curtains in her sitting room and settling into a favorite chair. She closed her eyes, called to mind the face of her coexperimenter, and asked herself over and over, "Where is he?" Then she wrote the description at right.

"Flight path? Red lights. Strong depth of field. Elmar seems detached, cold. A hole in the ground, a candle-shaped thing. Flower—maybe not real. Outdoors. See sky dark. Windy, cold. Something shooting upward." Immediately after the remote-viewing session, Schlitz added: "For some reason, a boat comes to mind. The impressions that I had were outdoors, and Elmar was at some type of—I don't know if institution is the right word—but some place. Not a private home or anything like that—something—a public facility. He was standing away from the main structure, although he could see it. He might have been in a parking lot or a field connected to the structure that identifies the place. I want to say an airport, but that just seems too specific. There was activity and people but no one real close to Elmar."

A Computer Test of Validity

Critics have long contended that early remote-viewing trials—including those of Puthoff and Targ or Schlitz and Gruber—relied too heavily on human judges whose personal biases and varying skill levels could skew the results. To address this complaint, in 1979 Robert Jahn, dean of the School of Engineering and Applied Sciences at Princeton University, and fellow psi investigators Brenda J. Dunne and Roger Nelson pioneered a new analysis technique that operated without judges.

The researchers provided their remote viewers and beacons with thirty standardized descriptive questions about the target, each of which could be answered only yes or no. After the session, the two sets of responses were digitized and entered into a computer, which quickly compared them not only with each other, but with the binary descriptions of the hundreds of other locations in the target pool. After 334 such trials involving some forty remote viewers, Jahn concluded there was little doubt that written descriptions like the one at right—of Urquardt Castle in Scotland *(below)*—contained "substantial pragmatic information."

"Rocks, with uneven holes, also smoothness. Height. Ocean—dark, dark blue. Whitecaps, waves— booming against rocks? On mountain or high rocks overlooking water. Dark green in distance. Gulls flying? Pelican on a post. Sand. A lighthouse? Tall structure— round with conical roof. High windows or window space with path leading up to it or larger structure similar to a castle. A black dog? With longish curly hair. Old, unused feeling; fallen apart? Musty or dank. Moss or grass growing in walls. Drawbridge?—wood. Ocean smells. Flowers? Snow ice—capping a mountain? High, large, cavernous hall—castle?"

"Anybody Can Do It"

In the early SRI trials, participants who had never experienced any psychic functioning were often judged to have described targets as accurately as subjects who had participated in many experiments. The finding led researcher Russell Targ to abandon the idea that remote viewing was anything but a democratic ability. "Anybody can do it," he says. "You just need to make your mind blank and receptive. Don't try to put a name on the place. Don't try to analyze where or what it is. Simply describe the shapes, the forms, the feeling of the place."

How well a person is able to do this, however, depends greatly on the environment in which he or she is asked to work, says Stephan Schwartz, director of the Mobius Society, a Los Angeles parapsychology research foundation. During the early 1980s, he and other psi researchers conducted a massive nine-month-long remote-viewing experiment in which photographs, rather than distant locations, served as targets. The pictures, randomly selected by computer from a seventy-two-image target pool, were projected inside a sealed box and changed every twenty minutes. The subjects, 3,300 people who responded to an ad placed in a magazine, were asked to draw an image that they felt matched the target. The participants were not pressured to conform to a rigid timetable; they were instructed to record their impressions whenever they chose to do so. According to Schwartz, the low-key protocol yielded results comparable to those of earlier remote-viewing experiments.

As this image of the Eiffel Tower was projected out of sight, one participant drew the scene below—in the subject's words, a "black iron" structure "steeper than a pyramid" possibly with "crenellations or carvings."

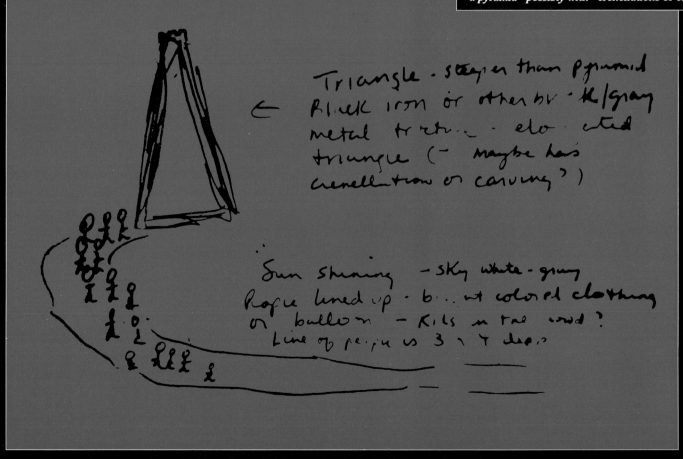

operated the device could pinpoint the location of a Soviet sub simply by putting its photograph into the machine. Ostensibly, the operator would then get a clear picture in his mind of the sub's whereabouts.

"It is possible to detect a submarine this way," asserted Captain Robert Skillen, then head of photographic research and development for the navy. Under his contract, Whitehouse provided training to several people from Skillen's department, some of whom had formerly served with the CIA. Skillen called Whitehouse's work "creditable," saying that in a test it brought searchers "into the area" where a submarine was hiding.

According to Whitehouse, sub chasing was only one of many uses for the versatile contraption. He also employed it to treat cancer patients, supposedly locating perforations and imbalances in their auras that could then be treated by illumination with colored lights. Whitehouse's machine allegedly had the potential to cure a number of other ailments, too. His manual for the analyzer even included a prescription for the aftereffects of "bombs (A and hydrogen)." Unfortunately for Whitehouse, such claims piqued the curiosity of investigators from the Virginia board

of medical ethics. Accused of defrauding patients, Whitehouse emigrated to Thailand, where he voiced the hope that "life will be more leisurely."

Whitehouse's abrupt departure was not the only embarrassment in the American psi-war effort in the late 1970s. Toward the end of the decade, according to reporter Ron McRae, the Office of Naval Intelligence tested as many as thirty-four psychics for their ability to track missile-carrying Soviet submarines—a vital capability not altogether within the navy's technological reach. One beneficiary of the new initiative was a Washington, D.C., palm reader, identified in published reports by the pseudonym Madame Zodiac. Every third Tuesday Madame Zodiac opened her parlor early for an unusual visitor—a navy commander dressed in civilian clothes and carrying a locked briefcase. The case held $400 cash for the palmist, a pack of photographs of Soviet subs, and ocean charts showing their estimated tracks near the east coast of the United States. The palmist was asked to confirm the submarines' current positions and to predict what they would do next.

Madame Zodiac's windfall lasted for eleven months during 1979 and 1980. The navy never released the results of the project. Indeed, its public affairs office flatly denied that psychics had ever been used to track submarines. Nevertheless, at least one leading figure in antisubmarine warfare remained convinced of the importance of such unconventional methods and did not mind saying so. In 1984, Ron McRae reported that Dr. Joel S. Lawson, Jr., a former head of the Naval Electronic Systems Command, had recently told McRae of his conviction, more than two decades old, that "ESP is the way to fight submarines."

Despite farcical encounters with con artists and palm readers, serious American fears about psychic progress on the other side of the Iron Curtain continued. One army colonel, John B. Alexander, raised the specter of Soviet use of psychotronics in a December 1980 article in the army publication *Military Review.* Surrounded by more conventional essays about new missiles and tactics, Alexander's article bore the title "The New Mental Battlefield: 'Beam Me Up,

Psychics Serving Uncle Sam

Defense contractors are common enough in American industry, but few provide the type of services offered by Psi Tech, an Albuquerque, New Mexico, corporation that says it supplies psychic expertise to military, government, and industry clients. Founded in 1989 by Edward Dames, a retired army major with intelligence experience, the company employs six psychics trained in what it calls "technical remote viewing."

According to Dames, the employees trained in remote viewing have the ability to "see" and precisely describe distant locations—including secret Iraqi biological and nuclear weapons sites, which he says were detected by Psi Tech through remote viewing in 1991. The company also reports using the procedure to spy on an automobile manufacturer's research-and-development facility, a task for which it was allegedly hired by a rival car company.

As Dames explains, technical remote viewing works not only over distance but also through time: One client, a "very large engineering company," hired the firm to document the mining techniques that will one day be used on the moon to extract oxygen from mineral deposits.

PSI TECH

"At Work in the Mind of Science"

Spock.'" Psychotronic weaponry, Alexander warned his fellow officers, would add a new dimension to battlefields that defied ordinary concepts of space and time.

Alexander's own belief in psychic powers, as he later wrote, had been strengthened by his combat experience in Vietnam. Throughout his tour as the commander of a Special Forces team, he credited his intuition with helping him survive the most dangerous missions. On a patrol deep into Vietcong territory, for example, Alexander said he suddenly felt the need to stop, for no logical reason. He then began backing up. Again, something made him pause. Looking down, Alexander realized that his boot was pulling back the trip wire for a booby trap. If he had backed up a few more inches, he recalled, he probably would have lost both legs.

In his 1980 article, Alexander admitted that the concept of psychotronic warfare "may stretch the imagination" but that nevertheless "research in this area has been underway for years, and the possibility for employment as weaponry has been explored. To be more specific, there are weapons systems that operate on the power of the mind and whose lethal capacity has already been demonstrated."

The American military's interest in psychotronic weaponry declined sharply during the 1980s, at least partly because of a withering barrage of adverse press reports. The age-old idea of psychic spying, however, remained alive and well. When Iranian revolutionaries took fifty-two American citizens hostage in the American embassy in Tehran in 1979, the National Security Council turned at one point to an SRI remote viewer to augment scanty intelligence on the condition of the hostages. The psychic, Keith Harary, homed in on one hostage he said suffered from a severe disease of the nervous system. This man, Harary predicted, would be released in July 1980. When that month came, the Iranians did indeed free Richard Queen, whose multiple sclerosis exactly fit Harary's description. Harary's seeming success led the NSC to authorize further work with Harary and Ingo Swann, both of whom supplied further impressions about the hostages' health and location.

The advent of the Reagan administration in 1981 gave new impetus to American military psi operations. Eager to achieve military parity with the Soviet Union in every field, the new president was also personally interested in astrology and open to other unconventional ideas. Under his administration, the CIA took renewed interest in parapsychology—and opportunities soon arose for psychics to perform on an international stage.

In December 1981, for instance, members of the Red Brigades, a notorious Italian terrorist organization, kidnapped American brigadier general James Dozier, then serving at the Verona NATO military command. Bursting into his Verona apartment, the kidnappers beat Dozier senseless, then bound and gagged his wife before bundling the general off in a large trunk.

Though officially a police matter, Dozier's abduction triggered a flurry of activity in the Italian and American military establishments. The Americans were particularly anxious to get the general back: Not only did Dozier hold topsecret information about the placement of troops and weapons throughout Europe, his kidnapping represented a direct challenge to the Reagan team, which had swept into the White House amid repeated campaign promises to get tough on terrorism.

While American officials pressured their Italian counterparts to step up the search for Dozier, the Pentagon mobilized its own forces in an operation dubbed Winter Harvest. Among the forces deployed, according to Steven Emerson, an investigator of covert military operations in the 1980s, were psychics supplied by two intelligence units.

The information those psi workers provided was augmented by a deluge of clues from self-described psychics across the United States. At least one of the volunteers seemed to have amazingly accurate knowledge, including facts that had not been released publicly, such as the position of Mrs. Dozier's earrings on the bathroom floor and the size of the trunk the kidnappers deposited the general in.

The psychic, whose first name was Gary, went on to win over skeptical Pentagon officials by accurately describing the layout of a nearby room he had never seen. For two days, Gary pored over maps and pictures of northern Italy, describing to his military hosts the house where he believed Dozier was being held as well as those places through which the captive NATO general had been moved. Unfortunately, this information—which was the crux of the investigation—was less accurate than the results of Gary's previous viewings; none of it proved useful to the searchers in Italy. Most of the leads from other psychics also turned out to be red herrings that consumed enormous amounts of official effort to check out.

Operation Winter Harvest continued, however, and several psychics were sent to Italy, including an unnamed American who had previously worked with police in California. After landing in the country, he confirmed his military escorts' worst fears when he refused to go to their Vicenza operations center until he had stopped in a local bar to treat the effects of jet lag. But the next day the psychic appeared to redeem himself in a meeting with an American intelligence officer and a representative of the Italian national police. Tersely, he described for them the place where he believed Dozier was being held: "I see a small house, made of stone. It is surrounded by a stone wall and a few trees. It has a tile roof and there is a road junction nearby and mountains in the background."

The description fit innumerable homes in northern Italy, but within a few days the Italians found what they believed to be the house in question. Under cover of darkness they concentrated 500 soldiers in the area behind stone walls and along nearby streets. At dawn, armed Italian police stormed into the house—and discovered, to the dismay of officials at all levels, an ordinary and extremely indignant Italian family, wholly innocent of any wrongdoing.

That morning's disastrous raid marked the end of psychic participation in Winter Harvest. Forty-two days after his kidnapping, Dozier was rescued by an Italian counterterrorist team, which had been led to a Padua apartment building by a combination of old-fashioned detective

A haggard General James Dozier (above), kidnapped by Red Brigades terrorists in December 1981, holds a blanket on which his captors wrote their demands. Held for forty-two days in a Padua apartment (right), Dozier was the object of an international search party that included psychics. Although their leads proved useless, seers will likely remain a part of the military's intelligence network.

work and high-tech intelligence methods.

Despite the failure of psychics to provide useful information in the Dozier case, the United States is believed to have used psychics in at least two other sensitive operations. On one occasion in either 1982 or 1983, several psychics allegedly aided an effort to plant electronic eavesdropping devices in the home of Panamanian dictator Manuel Noriega. After studying clandestine photographs of the heavily guarded villa, the psychics produced a two-page report on its layout and contents, including such details as the locations of bedrooms, guards, dogs, and security cameras. The information was never verified, however, and the remote viewers were clearly wrong about the canine aspect of the scene. Two agents sent to plant the bugs barely escaped capture, scrambling back over the garden wall after an unexpected encounter with vicious guard dogs.

The Pentagon also turned to psychics during Ameri-

ca's involvement in Lebanon during 1984. Again the object was a house, this one belonging to a suspected terrorist leader named Fadlallah. Hoping to mount a strike against Fadlallah with minimal harm to the rest of the neighborhood, counterterrorism experts asked a number of psychics to describe as much of the interior of his house as they could "see." Working only from a general description of the house, the psychics produced a report, describing such particulars as door locks and wall decorations and specifying the number of occupants. The report's sheer weight of detail supposedly astounded skeptical officials, yet in the end the information went largely unverified and unused.

Stepping back from such inconclusive psychic forays, a few American military thinkers have at times glimpsed a broader picture, in which today's halting efforts at psychic spying appear merely as the first steps toward a future when psi powers would be smoothly integrated elements in the military arsenal. One of the most detailed descriptions of how that might happen appeared in the 1970s, at a time when American military morale had reached a historic low.

The idea was put forward after the demoralizing conclusion of the Vietnam War, as the army cast about for new ways to train and motivate its troops. One source of new ideas was the Delta Force team, a loosely knit organization of 300 officers who came up with various highly innovative ideas. Some focused on sophisticated equipment to solve the army's problems; others emphasized developing human resources. Among the latter proposals was one for a unit manned by a new kind of soldier—a modern warrior-monk.

Members of the First Earth Battalion, as this psi-war unit was to be called, would be super soldiers, skilled not only in conventional combat methods but also in psi techniques such as levitation, psychic healing, and out-of-body travel. Communicating telepathically, they would go into battle with modern weapons but in the enlightened knowledge that strength of arms was the weakest of their powers. The most potent force in their arsenal would be love.

The idea for this most unlikely military unit sprang from the mind of Lieutenant Colonel Jim Channon, a Vietnam veteran with an art degree and graduate work in television journalism and systems analysis. Assigned by the Delta Force to investigate the human potential movement, Channon visited more than 130 New Age groups in California in the late 1970s. He combined what he learned from these groups with gleanings from martial arts masters, psychotherapists, theologians, and Eastern gurus to produce an eclectic manual for the First Earth Battalion.

The book, lavishly illustrated with Channon's own calligraphy and illustrations, sketched out the development of a warrior-monk from a variety of angles, most of them oblique. First Earth Battalion training would begin with a one-year curriculum emphasizing five areas, which Channon dubbed headwork, bodywork, biowork, heartwork, and psiwork. Headwork involved learning to clearly perceive life's problems. Bodywork stressed development of physical strength and skills, including yoga and the martial arts. Biowork was concerned with using foods and herbs to power the "mind-body instrument," while heartwork aimed at sustaining and using connections with other people. And psiwork involved studying consciousness, with the goal of transcending the material universe.

In psiwork, as in each of the other disciplines, the warrior-monk would pass certain milestones on the way to mastery. The first psi experience would be hearing and seeing another person's thoughts. More advanced practitioners would learn to travel out of their bodies at will and, later, to influence objects by thought alone. Trainees would eventually progress to passing unimpeded through walls. Ultimately, a master warrior-monk would be able to "slip the silver lining"—a haunting phrase that remained undefined.

Although the First Earth Battalion manual was similarly hazy on many subjects, it clearly envisaged a major shift in military thinking. Channon called for "uniforms without uniformity," and for networks of small teams that would arrive at decisions by consensus. Such suggestions only fueled antipathy among senior army officers reluctant to risk their careers for anything as profoundly unconventional as the First Earth Battalion. Despite a few high-ranking supporters, as well as reported interest from a conditioning coach for the Dallas Cowboys football team, the battalion was never elevated to operational status.

The fate of the First Earth Battalion, lost in a limbo of unofficial encouragement and official denial, illustrates the tug of war over any military application of psi powers. No military organization can afford to ignore the field, as long as there is even a slender chance that psychic ability can affect national security. In the interest of avoiding potentially devastating defeat, open-minded governments must monitor and analyze all the twists and turns of psi research—despite the possibility of occasional ridicule.

For parapsychologists, however, the choices are less clear. Many agree with Russell Targ, who left SRI because of what he viewed as excessive military involvement in psi research. Constrained by inevitable demands for secrecy, troubled by the ends to which their work might be put, these researchers would rather rely on civilian support, no matter how difficult it is to find. In the words of Richard Broughton, a researcher at the Institute of Parapsychology at Duke University, "psi ability, should it be understood and perhaps harnessed, must be reserved for helping and healing functions—not allied with weapons of destruction."

Hands-on Healers

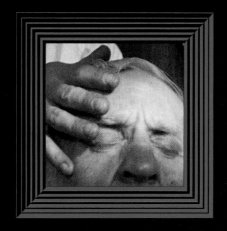

Le roi te touche, Dieu te guerisse.''
The king touches you, God cures you. With this formula and a touch of the royal hand, medieval French monarchs reportedly healed thousands afflicted with the tubercular disease scrofula. Also attributed to British sovereigns of the period, the alleged ability to cure stemmed from an age-old tradition of what many would call psychic healing—although then it was considered religious or magical power, as it often still is today. Whatever label it bears, priests, royalty, and common folk alike have practiced variations of psychic medicine from prehistoric times to the present.

Despite skepticism from the medical establishment, psychic healers enjoy increasing popularity among those who seek alternative therapies. Many healers credit divine power for their talents, saying they act as mere mediators between the patient and God; they are often known as faith healers. Others claim to be guided by otherworldly spirits. Practitioners of some ancient Asian healing arts say they restore well-being in their patients by directing the flow of cosmic energy that suffuses the universe. And yet others say they generate the life-giving energy from within. Nearly all healers rely on some form of touch *(above)* to effect their cures.

Whatever their method, most psychic healers—like those past and present who appear on the following pages—believe that sickness results from disharmony between an individual and the forces that govern body, mind, and soul. By restoring the natural harmony, they supposedly restore health.

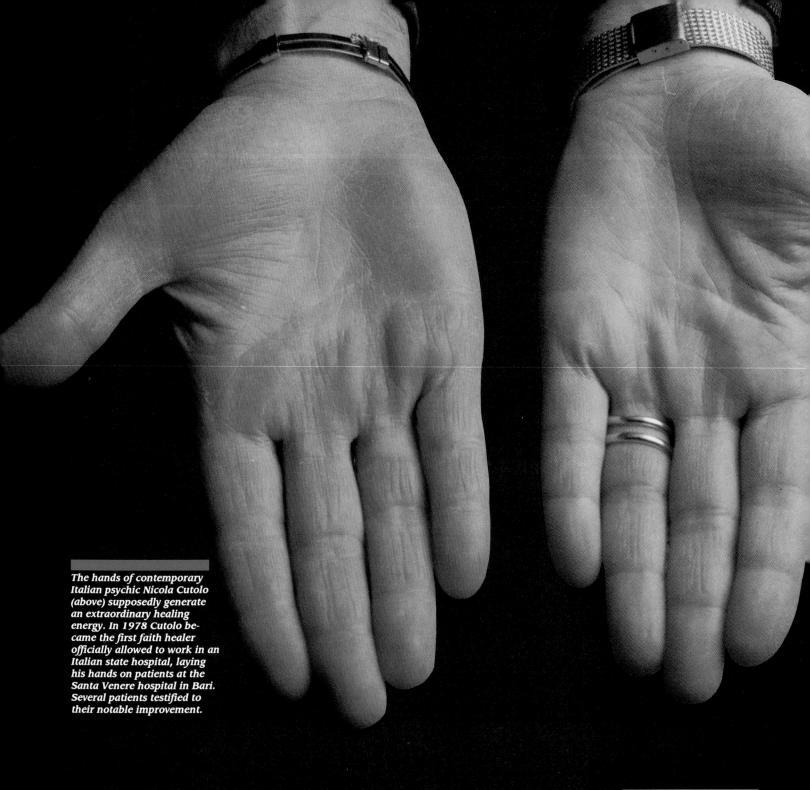

The hands of contemporary Italian psychic Nicola Cutolo (above) supposedly generate an extraordinary healing energy. In 1978 Cutolo became the first faith healer officially allowed to work in an Italian state hospital, laying his hands on patients at the Santa Venere hospital in Bari. Several patients testified to their notable improvement.

In this 1594 engraving, King Henry IV of France lays his hand on the brow of a sick man, one of more than 600 persons who gathered in Paris on Easter that year to be healed by the royal touch. In medieval days, the supernatural ability to cure certain diseases was considered irrefutable proof of a monarch's divine right to rule.

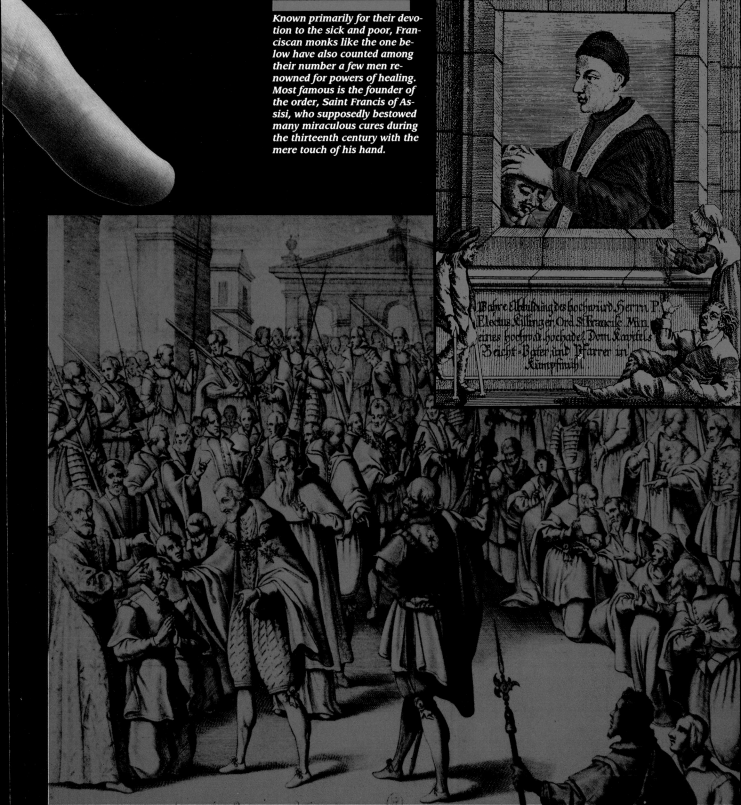

Known primarily for their devotion to the sick and poor, Franciscan monks like the one below have also counted among their number a few men renowned for powers of healing. Most famous is the founder of the order, Saint Francis of Assisi, who supposedly bestowed many miraculous cures during the thirteenth century with the mere touch of his hand.

Wahre Abbildung des hochwürd. Herrn P.
Electus Zillinger Ord: St Francisc: Min:
eines hochwürd: hochadel: Dom Capitels
Beicht-Vater und Pfarrer in
Kempfenhül.

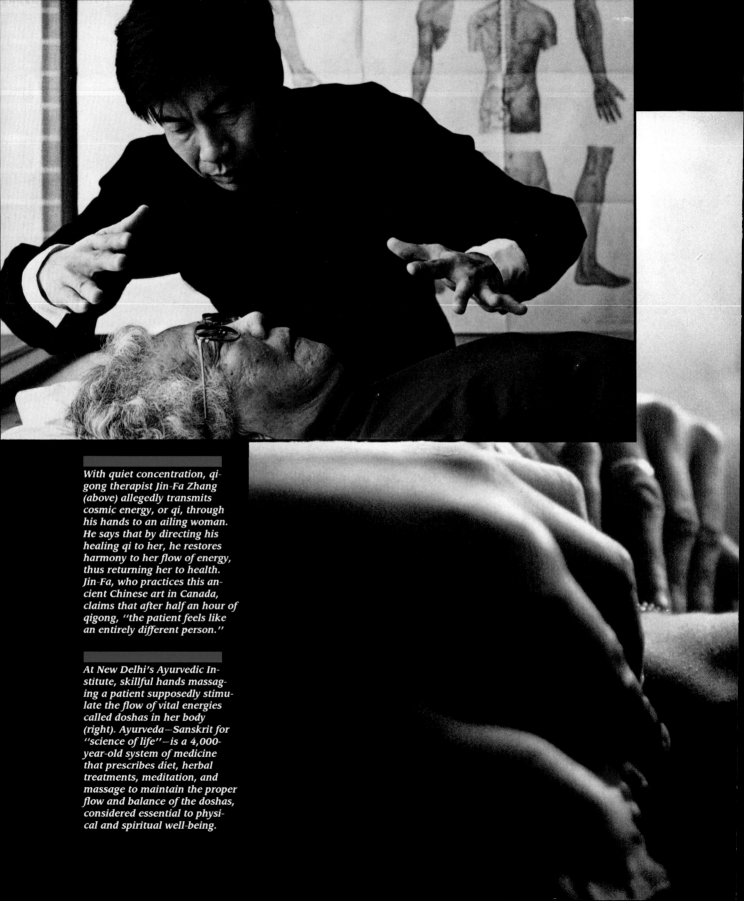

With quiet concentration, qigong therapist Jin-Fa Zhang
(above) allegedly transmits
cosmic energy, or qi, through
his hands to an ailing woman.
He says that by directing his
healing qi to her, he restores
harmony to her flow of energy,
thus returning her to health.
Jin-Fa, who practices this ancient Chinese art in Canada,
claims that after half an hour of
qigong, "the patient feels like
an entirely different person."

At New Delhi's Ayurvedic Institute, skillful hands massag-
ing a patient supposedly stimu-
late the flow of vital energies
called doshas in her body
(right). Ayurveda—Sanskrit for
"science of life"—is a 4,000-
year-old system of medicine
that prescribes diet, herbal
treatments, meditation, and
massage to maintain the proper
flow and balance of the doshas,
considered essential to physical and spiritual well-being.

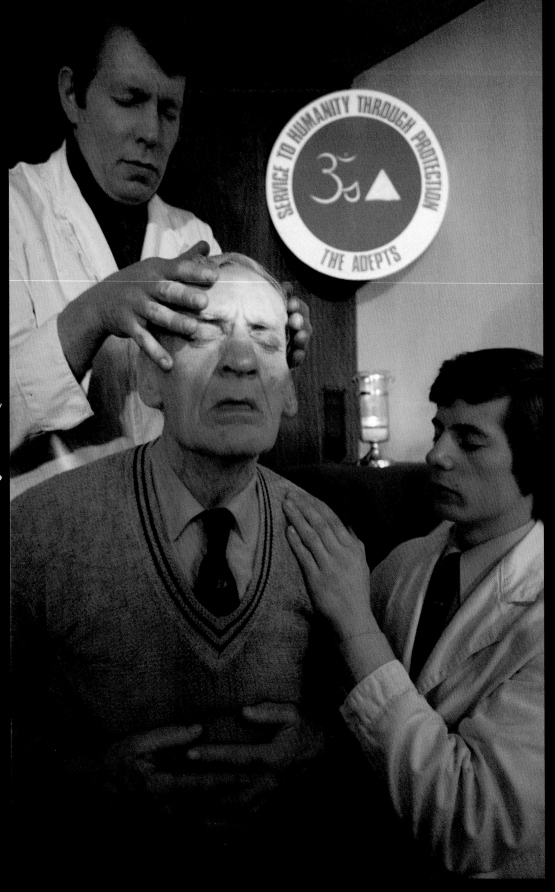

Through colored lights and touch, two Aetherius Society members try to restore a patient to health. Aetherians use green light, associated with harmony and balance, to make patients receptive to healing. The sect was founded in the 1950s by George King, an Englishman who believes everyone has the power to heal—one only needs to channel the universal life energies that flow from the sun. These energies, focused through prayer or a similar meditative act, can allegedly restore harmony and balance to an individual, to groups of people, or to the entire world.

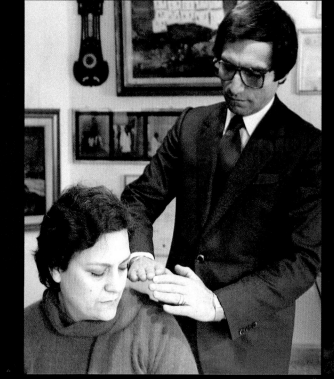

At right, psychic Nicola Cutolo spreads his palms above the arthritic shoulder of a client in an effort to saturate the area with vital energy. After seven or eight sessions, she was reportedly relieved of the affliction. Cutolo says there is nothing special about his hands as such, but that the power of his brain and his will propel a therapeutic current through the hands to his patients.

Afflicted by severe stomach cramps, a woman at Milan's Bio Chromo-Relax Institute (below) is bathed in colored light while therapists try to direct healing energy into her through their hands. The therapeutic use of colored lights—called chromotherapy—is said to assist the transfer of energy from the healer to the patient. This patient was pronounced cured after eight sessions.

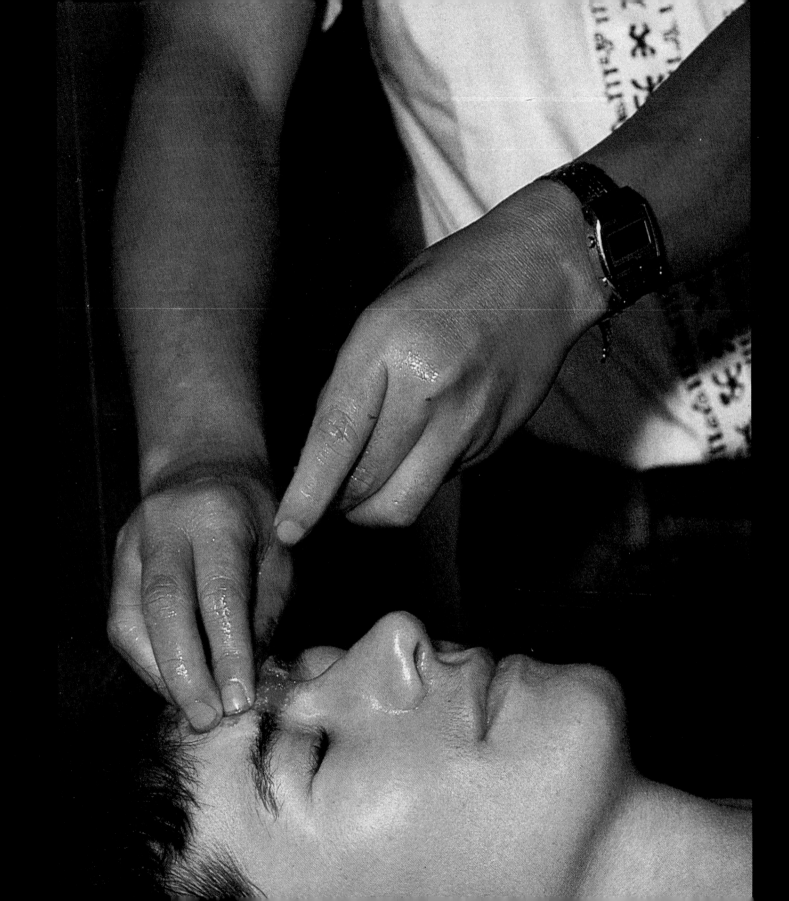

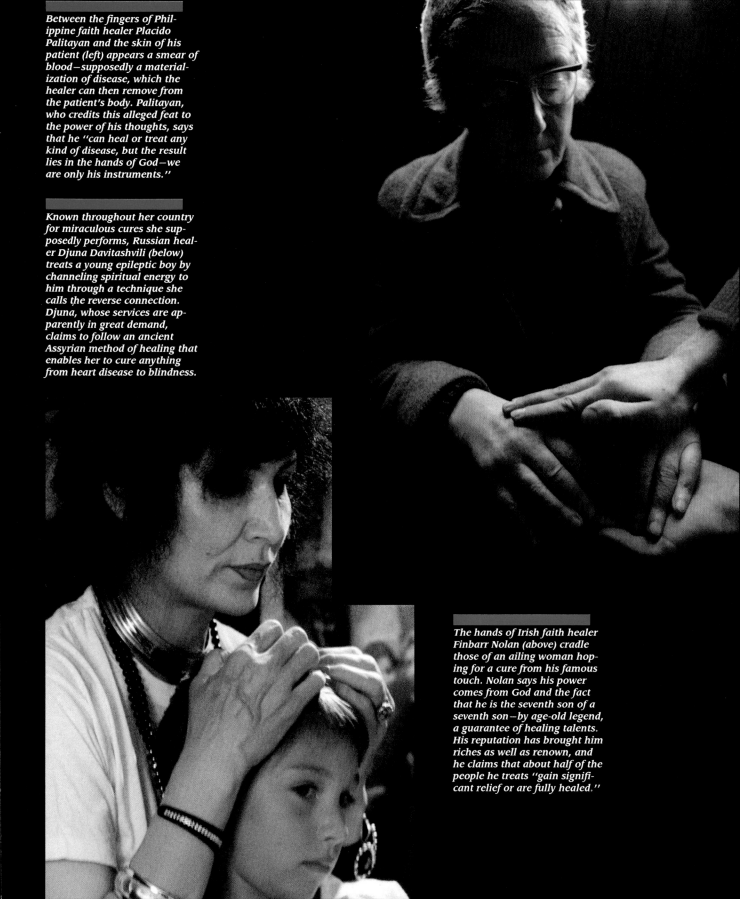

Between the fingers of Philippine faith healer Placido Palitayan and the skin of his patient (left) appears a smear of blood—supposedly a materialization of disease, which the healer can then remove from the patient's body. Palitayan, who credits this alleged feat to the power of his thoughts, says that he "can heal or treat any kind of disease, but the result lies in the hands of God—we are only his instruments."

Known throughout her country for miraculous cures she supposedly performs, Russian healer Djuna Davitashvili (below) treats a young epileptic boy by channeling spiritual energy to him through a technique she calls the reverse connection. Djuna, whose services are apparently in great demand, claims to follow an ancient Assyrian method of healing that enables her to cure anything from heart disease to blindness.

The hands of Irish faith healer Finbarr Nolan (above) cradle those of an ailing woman hoping for a cure from his famous touch. Nolan says his power comes from God and the fact that he is the seventh son of a seventh son—by age-old legend, a guarantee of healing talents. His reputation has brought him riches as well as renown, and he claims that about half of the people he treats "gain significant relief or are fully healed."

CHAPTER 3

Psychic Entrepreneurs

ay Kroc, owner of a Chicago industrial kitchen appliance company, was used to receiving large equipment orders from restaurants. But in 1952, when a small drive-in restaurant in San Bernardino, California, requested eight milk-shake machines, he was intrigued. It was a big order for such a small establishment, considering that each machine could mix five shakes at once. Kroc asked his West Coast salesman what the drive-in did with all those machines. "Well, Ray, they use them all," the salesman said. When an order came in for two more mixers, Kroc flew to California to see the restaurant for himself. "When I got there, I saw more people waiting in line than I had ever seen at any drive-in," Kroc later recalled.

Kroc immediately recognized that the two brothers who owned the restaurant, Richard and Maurice McDonald, were on to something big. Their drive-in offered a new type of food service that was fast and inexpensive and that appealed to young families—a rapidly expanding market in those postwar baby boom years. Within a few months Kroc had struck a deal with the McDonald brothers to franchise their restaurant nationwide. Within five years, the trademark golden arches could be seen at 228 McDonald drive-ins across the country. But under his contract, Kroc received less than 2 percent of the gross earnings of the restaurants and he had to relinquish a quarter of that to the brothers.

Because he was getting such a small return for his efforts and because he felt the McDonald brothers were not really supportive of the franchising concept, Kroc decided to buy them out a few years later. In 1961 he asked the brothers to quote him a price for the entire business, including the name. Their response: He could have everything, except the original San Bernardino restaurant, for $2.7 million. The brothers were not necessarily being greedy; they had done very well with their idea and wanted to come away from the sale with $1 million each after taxes.

But Kroc's lawyer thought it an exorbitant price, particularly since the original restaurant was not included; he advised his client to turn it down. Kroc himself was furious about the price; but something—some inner voice—kept him from walking away. "I'm not a gambler and I didn't have that kind of money, but my funnybone instinct kept urging me on," he recalled. "So I closed my office door, cussed up and down, and threw things out the window. Then I called my lawyer back and said: 'Take it!' "

Kroc's "funnybone" hunch turned out to be one of the most lucrative strokes of intuition in modern business history. Within a few years, the McDonald chain of drive-ins dominated the burgeoning fast-food industry, bringing in annual profits that dwarfed Kroc's original investment. Ray Kroc died in 1984 an enormously successful businessman. By the end of 1990, thirty years after Kroc accepted the McDonald brothers' buyout offer, the 11,803 restaurants in the chain had sold a total of 84.5 billion hamburgers—and an untold number of milk shakes.

Many successful businesspersons have made their fortunes following similar intuitive hunches. In 1906, for example, Wall Street wizard Jesse Livermore, well known for his uncanny ability to predict the stock market, acted on an impulse and sold Union Pacific stock short, although the railroad company was extremely sound financially. A few days later, on April 18, the great San Francisco earthquake struck, ravaging the city. Miles of Union Pacific track and tons of equipment were destroyed, and the company's stock plummeted. By acting on his inexplicable hunch, Livermore quickly netted more than a quarter of a million dollars, a huge sum in those days.

Tycoon Conrad Hilton also relied on intuitive feelings—or what his friends called "Connie's hunches"—to build his hotel empire. Once, for example, he decided at the last minute to increase his sealed bid for a prime piece of hotel property owned by the Stevens Corporation, a Chicago company. "My first bid, hastily made, was $165,000," he recalled. "Then somehow that didn't feel right to me. Another figure kept coming, $180,000. It satisfied me. It seemed fair. It felt right. I changed my bid to the larger figure on that hunch." When the bids were opened, Hilton's was found to be the highest by a mere $200. His intuition had won Hilton the bid—and the assets that came with it eventually netted him more than two million dollars.

Understandably, a skeptic might ask what these mysterious impulses have to do with psychic forces. The decisions made by Kroc, Livermore, and Hilton could have been just lucky hunches. Texas billionaire H. Ross Perot, who encourages his employees to follow their instincts, believes intuition is simply "knowing your business. It means being able to bring to bear on a situation everything you've seen, felt, tasted, and experienced in an industry." Indeed, an intuitive gamble in the business world may seem quite rational after it has succeeded. "What appears as a highly intuitive move at the time it is being made usually seems like common sense in retrospect," notes one executive.

Yet growing numbers of practical researchers—and businessmen and -women, too—believe that successful executives' intuition is more than a highly refined business sense. The researchers' evidence and the testimony of the executives themselves seem to

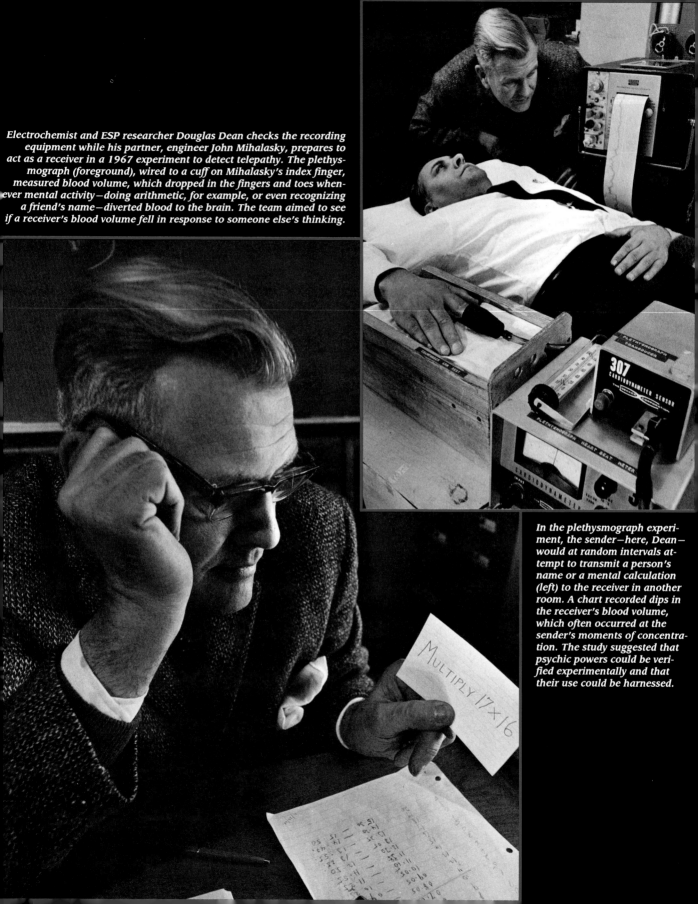

Electrochemist and ESP researcher Douglas Dean checks the recording equipment while his partner, engineer John Mihalasky, prepares to act as a receiver in a 1967 experiment to detect telepathy. The plethysmograph (foreground), wired to a cuff on Mihalasky's index finger, measured blood volume, which dropped in the fingers and toes whenever mental activity—doing arithmetic, for example, or even recognizing a friend's name—diverted blood to the brain. The team aimed to see if a receiver's blood volume fell in response to someone else's thinking.

In the plethysmograph experiment, the sender—here, Dean—would at random intervals attempt to transmit a person's name or a mental calculation (left) to the receiver in another room. A chart recorded dips in the receiver's blood volume, which often occurred at the sender's moments of concentration. The study suggested that psychic powers could be verified experimentally and that their use could be harnessed.

provide convincing evidence that some form of precognitive psychic power enables them to see into the future. There is also growing agreement that the capacity to tap into these extrasensory forces is not limited to a few spooky types with connections to the occult, but that it is a skill ordinary people can cultivate.

Two ardent proponents of the existence of "executive ESP" were physicists Douglas Dean and John Mihalasky. They studied the phenomenon in the early 1960s, when both men were teachers at New Jersey's Newark College of Engineering. Their research began during a three-day business conference in the Pocono Mountains. The two men asked sixty-seven company presidents to guess a 100-digit number that a computer would later select at random. The participants were divided into two groups: "strong dynamic" presidents, whom Dean and Mihalasky defined as "competitive, time-is-money, getting-things-done type people," and "strong nondynamics," whom the researchers called "mañana oriented in their attitude, putting things off until tomorrow."

The researchers found that the company presidents in the first, dynamic group averaged above chance on the precognition test, while those in the second, nondynamic group scored slightly below chance. Later Dean and Mihalasky compared the presidents' test scores with their ability to make profits for their companies. The researchers discovered that the presidents who had at least doubled their companies' profits scored 43 percent higher at precognition than did those who had amassed smaller profits.

Similar findings were reported more than a decade later by Weston Agor, a political-science professor at the University of Texas in El Paso, who tested the intuitive skills of 2,000 managers. In a study completed in 1982, Agor reported that top managers are much more skilled at using intuition for decision making than middle- and lower-level managers. He also found, incidentally, that women at all levels of management scored consistently higher than men at their ability to use intuition in the workplace, as did managers with Asian backgrounds.

When some of the executives in Agor's study were later questioned about their intuitive abilities, all but one acknowledged that they used intuition to guide their most important business decisions. "I do believe in using my intuitive powers on most of my decisions, large or small," said one executive. Researchers Dean and Mihalasky found a similar acceptance of intuitive decision making among the executives they tested. Asked whether or not they believed in ESP, forty-eight of the sixty-seven executives in that study—a ratio of three to one—said that they did. "I believe in ESP for one reason," said one of the presidents, "because I use it."

Many executives, however, feel uncomfortable openly using the term "ESP" to describe their business intuition. They prefer more acceptable terms, such as "hunch," "sixth sense," or "gut feeling." Some of these executives and the companies they work for are understandably reluctant to admit they encourage any psychic trafficking at all and insist on anonymity when discussing it. Agor, writing for the business newsletter *Boardroom Reports,* is quick to assure his mostly corporate audience (who might be put off by references to psychic phenomena) that "intuition is really a *logical* process . . . based partly on facts, partly on education and partly on experience—and feelings." Yet in his 1984 book *Intuitive Management,* Agor quotes psychologist Frances E. Vaughan, who defines intuition as "a way of knowing . . . recognizing the possibilities in any situation. Extrasensory perception, clairvoyance, and telepathy are part of the intuitive function."

Masatoshi Yoshimura agrees. A former president of Sanyo Chemical Industries, Ltd., in Tokyo, where the use of intuition in business dealings is taken for granted, Yoshimura believes "few people are gifted 'innately' with this supersensory perception. Yet even ordinary people can reach or get near to this level of ability through an intensive training. By placing oneself through a number of trials and overcoming them, one develops the ability to see things correctly, predict how others will behave, and decode messages received nonverbally. This ability is a form of insight, prediction, telepathy or precognition, all of which are products of an intricate working of the superconscious."

Despite the exaltation of rational process in Western thinking, intuition and its paranormal elements have not been completely overlooked. The seventeenth-century Dutch philosopher Baruch Spinoza described intuition as a "superior way of knowing ultimate truth without the use of prior knowledge or reason." In 1841, Ralph Waldo Emerson wrote: "The primary wisdom is intuition. In that deep force, the last fact behind which analysis cannot go, all things find their common origin. . . . We lie in the lap of immense intelligence. We are the receivers of its truth and organs of its activity." Of a more colloquial bent was the late American business philosopher R. Buckminster Fuller, who called intuition "cosmic fishing." He understood the problem most people have translating such out-of-the-blue flashes into useful action: "Once you feel a nibble," Fuller warned, "you've got to hook the fish." It is all too easy, he said, to

"get a hunch, then light up a cigarette and forget about it."

Most businesspersons who acknowledge that they use intuitive skills seem to agree that the skills involve an unconscious precognitive awareness of what is going to happen. "I get to feeling it right here," said William W. Keeler, former board chairman of Phillips Petroleum Company, pointing to his stomach, "and it is very strong. In fact, it sometimes is so strong I think of it as fact." Conrad Hilton described very much the same thing but in a different way. He would work through all the logical planning, then wait

William Kautz, whose San Francisco firm, the Center for Applied Intuition, provides "intuitive services" to major corporations, uses a group of well-known channelers to forecast not only business directions but also scientific discoveries, geopolitical situations, and trends in education and lifestyles. Predicted Kautz in 1987, "The whole area of applied intuition will be coming to great importance in the 1990s."

for an internal response: "When I have a problem and have done all I can to figure it, I keep listening in a sort of inside silence 'til something clicks and I feel a right answer."

In recent years, the United States business world has begun to act upon the growing conviction that intuition is a skill that not only can be used to competitive advantage, but that also can be learned. It may be some time before "corporate psychic" becomes a routine job description, but more and more companies quietly hire "expert intuitives" to train employees to use intuition on the job.

One such expert is William Kautz, founder of the Center for Applied Intuition (CAI) in San Francisco, a nonprofit organization dedicated to intuition research and training. Before establishing CAI in 1978, Kautz, a Massachusetts Institute of Technology graduate and computer scientist, had spent thirty-four years at a California research company, where he had been part of the team that designed the first mainframe computers. During the 1970s, Kautz's interest started to shift from computer science to the study of intuition. "I began to wonder where creativity comes from," he recalls. "So I started reading and was very surprised to find out that bright ideas were not the result of a lot of rational thinking—although that did play a role. But almost invariably, the scientists who made great breakthroughs got their ideas in a flash. This told me that there had to be some process going on in their minds that was generating information—not just reprocessing information already received. That process of direct knowing is intuition."

Kautz believes that understanding of intuition has been dismally neglected by Western societies, where rigid emphasis on objectivity and facts have blockaded access to powers of thought and perception—powers well known to ancient philosophers and embraced by many modern Eastern cultures. He suggests a model of the mind that has three concentric circles: The inner core of each human's consciousness is surrounded by a larger domain of personal subconscious, and the whole is enveloped by what he calls the "super-conscious," which is "the reservoir of all human knowledge and experience, actual and potential." Kautz's "super-conscious," like that of Japanese executive Masa-toshi Yoshimura, links all humans together. By clearing away the obstructions raised by our inflexible insistence on reason and logic, we can plug into this realm of higher consciousness that opens windows on the future.

Besides teaching business executives how to become more connected to the greater consciousness, Kautz also uses his own intuitive skills to advise the executives on what he sees for their companies' future—how well a new product will do, for example, or whether or not a company should be expanding into new markets. These judgments Kautz describes as prophecies of broad social forces and directions as opposed to specific psychic predictions. Yet Kautz's own predictive abilities have made him appear remarkably psychic. Once, while fielding questions from the president and other board members of a large Japanese retail company, Kautz experienced a sudden and uneasy thought: He sensed that someone in the room had been siphoning off company funds. Kautz mentioned it to the men and even provided details of how the embezzler had diverted money from company accounts to his own. The board members were horrified. Immediately after the meeting the president launched an investigation, which did, indeed, uncover an embezzler.

Although public acceptance of the idea that psychic abilities may con-

Millionaire stock trader Jesse Livermore, shown here with the first of his three wives, used his apparent precognitive skills to turn a ten-dollar stake into holdings that included an apartment on New York's Park Avenue, a Long Island estate, and a private railroad car. Unfortunately, his powers abandoned him just before the disastrous stock market crash of 1929.

tribute to financial or business success is a modern trend, the phenomenon itself has been a recurrent theme in the business world. Indeed, some of history's most famous business people often relied on psychics to back up their own hunches. Nineteenth-century American financiers Cornelius Vanderbilt and J. P. Morgan both consulted clairvoyants and fortunetellers. Oil billionaire H. L. Hunt often turned to a psychic to help him make multimillion-dollar deals. And entertainment tycoon Walt Disney is rumored to have used an astrologer to time the signing of business contracts and the introduction of new Disney products onto the market.

The most unforgiving testing ground of financial ESP abilities may be the stock market, and many's the scheme tried by hopeful players that has failed miserably. But some speculators, using strategies with no apparent grounding in logic or reason, have had such sensational successes, so far exceeding the limits of probability and chance, that a belief in their psychic powers is hard to resist. Jesse Livermore, the Wall Street wizard who followed his intuition and made a bundle by selling Union Pacific stock short, showed an exceptional talent for predicting the stock market.

The son of a poor Massachusetts farmer, Livermore went to Boston as a teenager and took the first job that came his way—clerk in a brokerage house. According to journalist Max Gunther in his 1971 book *Wall Street and Witchcraft,* Livermore quickly discovered he had a knack for guessing the rise and fall of stocks. Soon, for the fun of it, he began recording his stock forecasts by drawing tiny arrows pointing up or down on the chalkboard where his firm displayed the current stock price quotations. His bosses at the brokerage firm expressed first amusement, then astonishment at the accuracy of the clerk's forecasts.

"Good heavens, young man!" one elderly gent told him in 1893. "If I were right as often as you, I could buy the entire city of Boston! How do you do it?"

"I don't know, sir," Livermore replied. "It's just a feeling I get from watching a stock go up and down. After a while I seem to know which way it ought to go next."

When the brokerage firm asked him to stop drawing his arrows (the bosses feared rumors their firm was dabbling in the occult), Livermore decided to test his hunches with real money. He borrowed ten dollars from a fellow employee and put it into Burlington Railroad stock. When he sold the stock a few days later, he had made three dollars in profit. After paying back his friend, Livermore reinvested the three dollars and quickly doubled it. Within a very short time, he ran up that small stake to more than $2,500. Recognizing then that his forecasting ability was not a fluke,

sound sleep difficult. Something would jog me into consciousness. . . . Something sinister would seem impending. . . ."

Curiously, Livermore's precognitive sense of the stock market failed him in his later years. Early in October 1929, Livermore felt uneasy about the market but had no clear vision of what to do. "I must be getting old," he told a friend. "I don't feel sure of myself any more. I have a feeling the stock market is going to make big news this month. I feel some kind of tension gathering. But I don't know whether to go short or long."

So Livermore did nothing. A few weeks later, on October 29, Wall Street's notorious Black Tuesday, came the worst crash in the market's history. Livermore lost everything and eventually had to declare bankruptcy. During

Livermore decided to quit his job in Boston and go to New York to become a full-time market player on Wall Street. He was twenty-one years old.

Years later, in his autobiographical book, *How to Trade in Stocks,* Livermore tried to explain his seemingly irrational ability to predict the ups and downs of Wall Street. "There would come a time," he wrote, "when, after the market closed, I would become restive. That night I would find

the next decade, he struggled to rebuild his empire with a small stake borrowed again from a friend. But as he himself admitted, he had lost "it"—and the new stake soon disappeared. Broke and despondent, the sixty-two-year-old former tycoon walked into a New York hotel bar one cold afternoon in December 1940, ordered two old-fashioneds, then went into the men's room and shot himself.

Others who have played the stock market successfully

have been more specific about crediting their psychic abilities. T. O. Tulley was a retired widower who decided in the late 1950s to risk what was left of his savings, some $3,000, on the market. As told by journalist Gunther, Tulley had felt as a child that he had psychic powers—he'd know what someone was going to say before the words came out, for instance—and as he approached old age he decided it was time to put his mysterious abilities to work.

Following his hunches, Tulley bought and sold stock with astonishing success. In 1958, for example, he bought Inland Steel stock at twenty-five dollars a share, then sold it at fifty-three dollars a year later; in 1962, he bought Kinney National stock at nine dollars, then sold it at twenty-two dollars in 1963—right before the stock slid back down to fifteen dollars. By 1970, Tulley had turned his small savings into an impressive $800,000.

Tulley, who lived in a modest hotel on Manhattan's East Side, walked down to Wall Street just about every day to pick up "the aura," as he called it—an inexplicable sense of what was going to happen next in the stock market. "My theory is that what I've got here is some kind of mass telepathy," he once told a reporter. "You see, anything that's going to happen on the market tomorrow is pretty well decided right now in people's minds. . . . The numbers that come out on the tape every day are the result of what people have been thinking the previous day, the previous week and month. So if you have some way of knowing what people are thinking—if you can gauge the sum total of all those millions of thoughts—then you know roughly what the numbers on the tape are going to be."

Tulley considered his head to be "a kind of receiving station" for all those millions of thoughts. Thus, as he took his daily walk down Wall Street, he would "listen" to his intuitive feelings—and then call his stock broker with specific instructions about which stocks to buy or sell. He claimed to have been seldom wrong.

Many people without such faith in their own hunches have turned to psychics for advice on playing the market. In 1967, *Newsweek* magazine reported that several dozen Chicago investors were following the tips of psychic Olof Jonsson. "Jonsson runs his finger down a newspaper stock table and, when he gets a special sensation, stops and writes down the name of the stock," noted *Newsweek*. Jonsson reportedly led the investors to a number of small, little-known stocks that quickly doubled or quadrupled in worth.

In New York, psychic Shawn Robbins told an interviewer in 1988 that she advises five to ten small investors a week. The forty-six-year-old Robbins, who says that both her mother and grandmother were psychic, comes by her advice through dreams, visions, and good old-fashioned common sense. Although she claims to be making money on the stock market, some of her other predictions—made on local radio shows and in her 1980 autobiography *Ahead of Myself: Confessions of a Professional Psychic*—have fallen flat. "The truth is this psychic phenomenon is anything but an exact science," Robbins says frankly. "I'm simply wrong sometimes."

Robbins may be willing to admit psychic powers are not grounded in science, but not so Keith Harary, a San Francisco psychologist and psychic who in 1982 helped a group of investors earn more than $120,000 on the silver market. Harary undertook the project, which was reported on the PBS television series *Nova,* not just to make money for the investors, but also to prove a scientific point. He and two colleagues, physicist Russell Targ and businessman Anthony White, had recently formed Delphi Associates, named for the site of the famous Greek oracle, where questioners sought the advice of the gods. The organization's purpose was to help business people apply their innate psychic powers to their work. The three men wanted to see if the psychic procedure known as remote viewing, which seemingly involved precognitive abilities, could be used to predict changes in the stock market.

The silver futures experiments were conducted over nine weekends, according to an intricate system worked out by the associates. Each Thursday morning, Targ was to

Counsel in the Cards

"With business, I always use the Tarot," says Arizona psychic Anita Smith *(left)*. "It's more objective." Smith offers advice to clients concerned about the stock market, the timing of investments, or whether to take on a business partner. In response to this last question, the Tarot spread at left, she says, gives a go-ahead.

In the top row, she says, "the center card is the issue"; the Sun signifies reaching the goal. To its left is the recent past: The Ace of Wands means good timing, but the card is inverted. This signals an obstacle, revealed by the leftmost card: The Star means "you want to go it alone even when you shouldn't." To the Sun's right is the future: The Five of Wands shows the querent "fighting even when you don't need to." Next, the inverted Empress represents "hidden fears about dealing with a strong woman"— the prospective partner, perhaps.

In the second row, says Smith, the inverted Seven of Swords *(far left)* warns against quarrelsomeness. The inverted Three of Cups *(center)* refers to difficulty trusting others, but its position under the Sun shows this is the time to do it. The last card in the row, the inverted Eight of Swords— depicting a woman who looks trapped but is free to go—is a reminder that "agreements can be changed." The last card in the spread reveals the final outcome: "If it's upside down, the project is a bad idea," counsels Smith. In this spread, the Lovers—"the optimum partnership card—means it's an excellent time to go into partnership."

call Harary at his apartment and ask him to describe an object that Harary envisioned being delivered to him the following Monday afternoon, after the financial markets had closed. Targ would then call White and ask him to randomly choose four common objects in his home, such as a pencil or a pie pan, to represent one of four possible movements in the silver market: up or down less than twenty-five cents, and up or down more than twenty-five cents. After White had made his choices, Targ would then describe Harary's envisioned object, and the two men would decide if the description matched any of the four objects White had chosen. If it did not, the session was declared a "pass." But if it did, Targ would call their broker and tell him to either buy or sell silver, depending on which object had been described. Then on Monday, after the actual price fluctuations of the silver market were known, the object that represented those fluctuations would be delivered to Harary.

During each of the nine successive trials, Harary's envisioned object matched one of White's chosen objects, thereby "predicting" the market's fluctuation over the weekend. Most importantly, in each case the market did indeed follow the prediction—and the investors made money. Thus Harary had successfully "seen" into the future, forecasting on each of the nine Thursdays what the state of the silver market would be on the following Monday.

"The pressure was intense," Harary later recalled. "I was able to keep very calm and clear while doing it but I wouldn't want to keep that particular pace up indefinitely. That's to say, I think it requires a rest after a while." Indeed, a later attempt to duplicate the experiments failed. By then, Harary had become tired and bored with the project, he said, and, as a result, was experiencing displacement, a common problem in psychic experiments in which the "viewer" still gets mental impressions of objects but the images do not necessarily relate to the experiment at hand.

Still, the Delphi Associates insist that the later failures in no way negate the original successes but merely point up how important it is to continue exploring their remote frontier. "You have to show that psychic abilities are useful,"

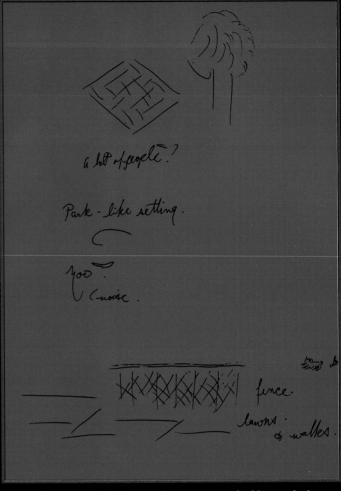

"I can smell the peanuts. Is it the zoo?" asked parapsychologist Keith Harary, a receiver in a March 1983 remote-viewing trial. Harary, busily sketching his impressions of a location unknown to him (above), was taking part in what would be one of the final experiments administered by the psi investigators Delphi Associates.

Just four months earlier, Delphi Associates had attempted to predict the movement of silver futures through precognitive remote-viewing trials. Although the nine initial experiments were successful, Harary characterized them as "not careful science." Thus when the group reconvened in March to continue the experiments, they instituted a stricter set of double-blind controls.

In earlier remote-viewing experiments, Harary had been asked to identify an object that he believed Targ would hand him on a given day in the future; for the new trials, Harary would try to visualize a place that he and an associate would visit a few days hence. A pool of four possible destinations would be chosen after Harary recorded his impressions, by a researcher working in isolation. Each location, like the objects used in the earlier trials, represented a fluctuation in the silver market—a change up or down of up to twenty-five cents or exceeding twenty-five cents.

When Harary began remote viewing the first location, he noted that he was seeing a zoo. Realizing that he was making the classic psi-trial

Harary points out in explaining the associates' dedication to their work. "We must establish the reality of psychic functioning not only in the scientific journals but in the *Wall Street Journal*." Further exploration that is both imaginative and precise may well develop remote viewing into a reliable stock market oracle, but the odds against its being readily accepted in this skeptical society are still high. The same goes for two other ancient psychic arts that have occasionally been called on in speculators' abiding passion to beat the market: the Tarot and witchcraft.

In the Tarot, the practitioner relies on seventy-eight pictorial cards to suggest answers to specific questions, such as what direction a particular stock will take. No scientific studies have been conducted to test the Tarot's effectiveness in picking winning stocks, but several anecdotes about people using the cards to build small fortunes have circulated from time to time on Wall Street. Max Gunther, in his *Wall Street and Witchcraft,* tells of a man who walked into stockbroker Marty Tressler's Beverly Hills office one afternoon in 1966 with a check for just under $5,000—the man's entire savings. He wanted to put it all into the stock of a little-known Minneapolis-based company called Con-

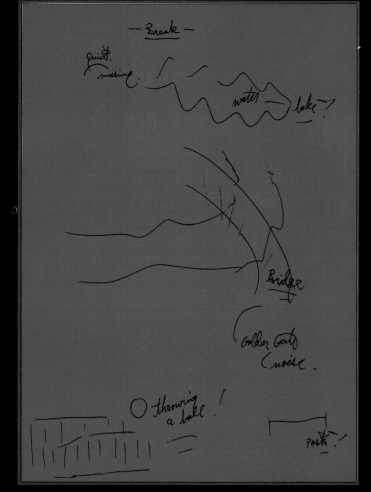

mistake of interpreting his impressions rather than simply describing them, he wrote the word "noise," a term the researchers used to indicate an interpretation. Harary then continued to concentrate for some time, and filled three pages with scenes he sensed precognitively, such as ball throwing, fences, water, a bridge, and a curvy road.

When the viewing session was over, Targ and White set about deciding what location Harary's drawings represented. Although they claimed not to have been influenced by the receiver's initial interpretation of the images as a zoo, the judges decided after careful scrutiny of the sketches that they did indeed represent a local zoo, one of the four possible target sites. A trade was made on the silver market

based on the price movement that corresponded to the zoo location; it proved to be a bad investment. Had the judges determined that the drawings resembled the Malibu Miniature Golf (far left), as Harary felt they should have, the trade would have been profitable.

The associates were disheartened by the results but continued the experiment for one more trial. The second attempt also resulted in a trading loss. Delphi Associates soon disbanded, although the former partners have not given up on the idea that remote viewing can become a useful tool in the business arena. They concede that the misses "certainly motivated us to do further research before returning to the marketplace."

trol Data, whose shares had been drifting downhill in value for almost three years. When Tressler asked the man why he wanted to risk all his money on such a troubled stock, the man muttered "Tarot," and disappeared.

With serious reservations about the wisdom of the transaction, Tressler did as the man said and put the $5,000 into Control Data stock, which was selling at around $30 a share. To Tressler's amazement, the stock soon began to rise at a dizzying rate, reaching a height of $165 per share within six months. At that point, the Tarot practitioner returned to Tressler's office to cash in his stock, which was

then worth more than $60,000. He had triple-quadrupled his original investment. Tressler never saw the man again.

Psychics who use Tarot cards to play the stock market are trying to predict which way the market will go. Some witches, on the other hand, have used their psychic powers to try to influence the market's direction. Again, Gunther has a story to tell. He writes that he attended a meeting of a witches' coven during which participants focused their powers on getting a particular stock to rise in the coming week. "The idea is to put a certain stock in a lot of investors' minds, so they'll buy it and the price will rise," a male

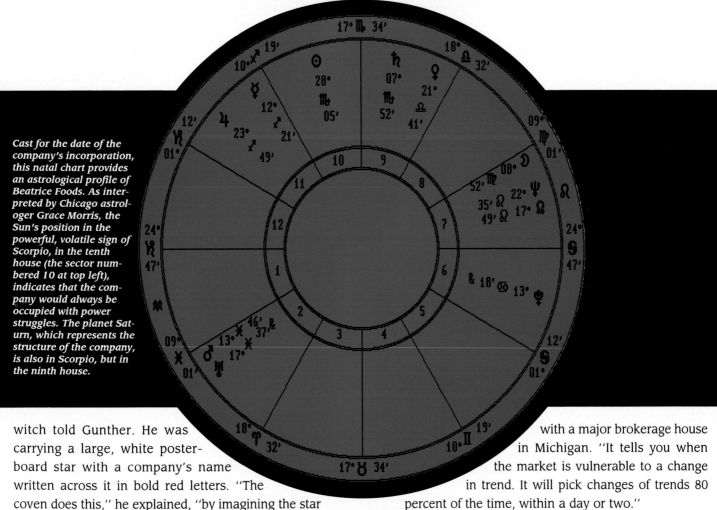

witch told Gunther. He was carrying a large, white posterboard star with a company's name written across it in bold red letters. "The coven does this," he explained, "by imagining the star hanging in a dark sky, huge and shining . . . with the company's name standing out in red." The following week, that company's stock gained 5⅛ points, or 25 percent. The witches, according to Gunther, having bought 500 shares of the stock, made $2,500 profit in just five days.

Remote viewing, witchcraft, and Tarot readings lurk on the far fringes of acceptability for most stock market players and business people. Astrology, on the other hand, has become a nearly respectable source of guidance for many brokers and traders. These professionals listen to the suggestions of a small but growing band of counselors who call themselves astro-economists. Practitioners of this discipline do not consider themselves psychic; nor do they believe their work has anything to do with the occult. They simply believe that the movements of the stars and planets release energies that affect all human-related activity on earth, including stock market activity.

Astro-economists may not think of themselves as psychics, but to the uninitiated, their cryptic language and esoteric theories give off an otherworldly aura. For those who believe, though, astro-economics is all business. "I use astrological configurations for timing," notes a vice president

with a major brokerage house in Michigan. "It tells you when the market is vulnerable to a change in trend. It will pick changes of trends 80 percent of the time, within a day or two."

Like the use of psychics in business affairs, the notion of linking the stars with market fluctuations is hardly new. One of the first to successfully use astrology for buying and selling stock was the mystic W. D. Gann. Born in the cotton-growing town of Lufkin, Texas, on June 6, 1878, Gann first began playing the cotton market at age twenty-four, using a system based on Babylonian, Egyptian, and Chaldean astronomy, and other ancient sources, including the Bible and *Elements,* a great mathematical treatise by the Greek Euclid. In 1908, Gann moved to New York City, where he set up a brokerage office at 91 Wall Street and began to use his charting method to trade on dozens of markets, from onions to oil.

Gann created an instant sensation on the Street. In December 1909, a financial newsletter, *The Ticker and Investment Digest,* described Gann's amazing skills. "During the month of October, 1909, in 25 market days," reported the newsletter, "Mr. Gann made, in the presence of our representative, 286 transactions in various stocks, on both the long and short side of the market; 264 of these transactions resulted in profits; 22 in losses. The capital with which

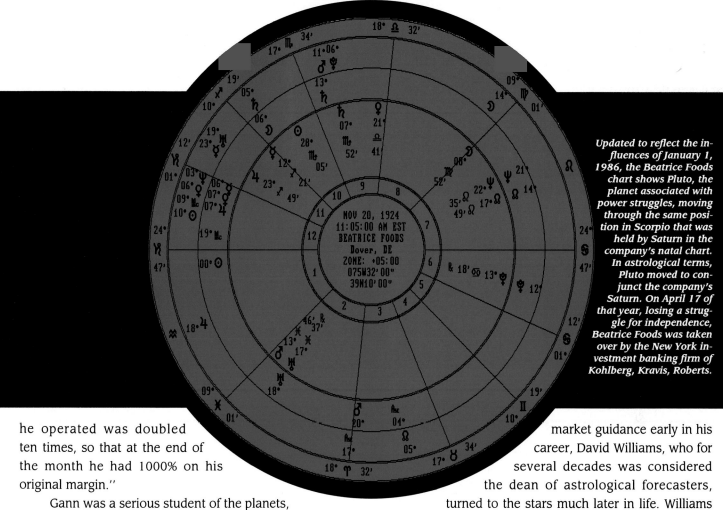

he operated was doubled ten times, so that at the end of the month he had 1000% on his original margin.''

Gann was a serious student of the planets, but he included a whole range of natural phenomena in what he called the ''Natural Law of Vibration.'' The law governed all events on earth, Gann argued, including the ups and downs of the stock market. And like other natural laws, it could be mathematically calculated and thus used to forecast the future. From the Law of Vibration, Gann determined that the markets are cyclical and that the amount of time a particular stock is down is directly proportional to how long it remained at its previous high and what its price was at that high. ''Everything in existence is based on exact proportion and perfect relationship,'' he wrote. ''There is no chance in nature because mathematical principles of the highest order lie at the foundation of all things.''

Gann described his system for determining the cycles of the various markets in numerous books and papers, but his writing style was so obtuse that his methods have proven difficult for most of his followers to decipher and duplicate. Still, those who can understand his strange and complicated teachings continue to follow them avidly, assisted by elaborate computer software programs—and inspired, perhaps, by the fact that when Gann died in June 1955, he had earned in excess of $50 million on Wall Street.

While Gann came to rely on the heavens for stock market guidance early in his career, David Williams, who for several decades was considered the dean of astrological forecasters, turned to the stars much later in life. Williams was past fifty when, in the mid-1950s, he became intrigued with the idea that solar disturbances, caused perhaps by the motions of planets, might influence earthly phenomena. Williams was working as an executive engineer for the Consolidated Edison power company in New York City. His responsibilities included projecting how much cable his company would need for several years in the future, and then buying the cable at the lowest possible price.

Williams used standard economic-forecasting methods to determine when to buy the cable, but unpredictable market factors, such as strikes and wars, made his job very difficult. He began to search for new ways of predicting the market. That's when he chanced upon several scientific studies indicating that sunspots might be influencing a variety of happenings on earth, from slowing down the growth of trees to changing weather patterns. Williams also noted that some scientists speculated—erroneously, it turns out—that the formation of the sunspots was caused by the gravitational pull of the planets. The more Williams read about the planetary influence on the sun and its possible impact on the earth's magnetic environment, the more he wondered if celestial disturbances could not also be causing subtle changes in the tiny electric impulses that flash through the human brain. Such changes might be influencing people's moods, he reasoned, making them irritable and pessimistic at certain times—and perhaps unable to make good judgments about the stock market.

"It was just a wild theory at first," Williams later recalled. "I didn't really expect it would amount to anything." But after checking historical records back to the 1700s, Williams claimed to find evidence that, with only a few exceptions, certain planetary patterns had coincided repeat-

edly with specific market movements. "I have tracked this theory through almost 200 years of American financial history," he said, "and have found, for instance, that the single most accurate indicator of market lulls is the pattern called the Mars-Jupiter Conjunction, which occurs at approximately four- to four-and-a-half-year intervals."

From his research, Williams also discovered that the great stock market crash of 1929 had been correctly predicted by many astrologers, including J. P. Morgan's full-time

To develop forecasts for his monthly Astro-Market Letter, published from his home in Wetter, Germany, astro-economist Hans Gerhard Lenz (above) compares business and stock market horoscopes with the positions of the planets. Investors may be dubious, Lenz notes, "but when they realize they can make money with astrology, anything goes."

As president of Astrolabe, a company named for a medieval celestial navigation instrument, Robert Hand (left) offers modern investors a new way to steer by the stars. Astrolabe's software package calculates and displays in graph form (superimposed on photograph, left) "astro indicators" for every facet of market trading.

stargazer, Evangeline Adams. Morgan had fortunately heeded his astrologer's advice, Williams noted, selling much of his stock portfolio before the crash.

Williams eventually left Consolidated Edison to follow the stars and the stock market. He claimed that by using his own celestial readings he roughly doubled his money every three years. Nor was his precognitive prowess confined to the stock market. While at a party on August 4, 1960, for example, Williams made a prediction that seemed so unlikely to his friends that they wrote it down on a piece of paper, then signed and dated it. Three years later, the prediction tragically came true. For on that warm August evening Williams had prophesied that John F. Kennedy would be elected president—and that he would die in office.

Since 1965, Williams has published his stock market predictions regularly in *Horoscope* and other magazines. Today, many practitioners of astro-economics offer financial advice to clients through newsletters and daily "hotline" telephone numbers, which clients can call to get the very latest astrological readings about various markets and stocks. One of the most impressive of these has been "Crawford Perspectives," published by a leading member of the new generation of astro-economists, Arch Crawford.

Crawford studies and interprets a variety of atmos-

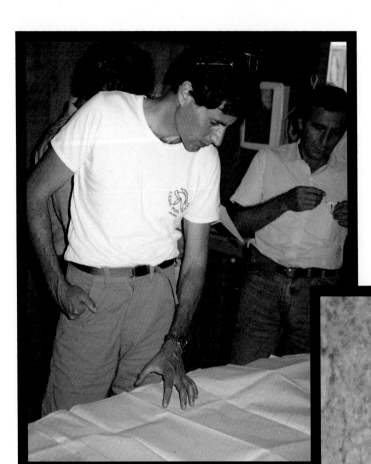

pheric conditions, such as sunspots and ionospheric storms, as well as planetary positions when making his market predictions. He cites the historical record for this conviction: In 1878 (the same year W. D. Gann was born) British economist William Stanley Jevons read a paper entitled "The Periodicity of Commercial Crises and Its Physical Explanation." The text points out a correlation between the sunspot cycle and the price of wheat.

Crawford does not predict the up and down movements of individual stocks, just market trends. He has had some stunning successes. In February 1985, *Business Week* reported that Crawford had been one of the handful of Wall Street brokers who had correctly predicted the big bull mar-

Famed spoon bender and psychic consultant Uri Geller passes his hands over a map of Brazil's Amazon region, preparing to instruct officials of a Japanese mining firm where to dig for gold. When he begins to feel "magnetic sensations" during map dowsing, Geller says, the next step is a flight over the site for "aerial hand dowsing."

Multimillionaire Geller flashes a smile amid a somber crew of South African gold miners, during one of his infrequent visits to the site of a dig. He claims a high success rate in psychically locating deposits of precious commodities but says most clients insist on anonymity.

ket that began a month earlier, on January 10. Three years later, *Money* magazine also noted that Crawford had correctly warned his investors to get out of the stock market just days before the precipitous October 1987 crash.

Eclipses, Crawford claims, are important indicators of market trends. "Lunar eclipses tend to bring out bank failures and denote downward market trends and the end of speculative phases," he explains, "while solar eclipses signify monetary changes." Crawford and other astro-economists tellingly point out that at the time of the solar eclipse on July 22, 1990, the Dow Jones averages on the New York Stock Exchange dropped 125 points; two weeks later, right after a lunar eclipse on August 6, the market fell another 95 points. Crawford also believes that sunspot activity causes people's electromagnetic fields to reach a "high positive" ionization in January and a "high negative" ionization in July. These ionization patterns affect people's moods which, in turn, affects the market, he says. "Whether one feels confident or unconfident varies from person to person," Crawford points out, "but there is a tendency for the market to reach highs in April and lows in October."

Chicago psychotherapist and professional astrologer Grace Morris takes a more specific astrological approach to stock market concerns. She finds out a company's date of incorporation before making any prognostications about the future of that company and its stock. She uses the com-

pany's incorporation date to chart its horoscope, then searches the horoscope for indications of future times when the sun and planets will be lined up either favorably or unfavorably. If favorable times are approaching, she advises her clients to buy the company's stock; if unfavorable times seem imminent, she cautions them to sell.

Morris also consults with companies directly, helping them determine the best astrological time to sign contracts, schedule important meetings, expand product lines, or make other business decisions. "People are very unaware of how many events happen in relation to astrological signs," says Morris. (She believes, for example, that the new moon is usually an exceptionally good time for starting new business ventures.) Morris has also been a prime mover in a crusade to bring respectability to her vocation. Besides developing astrological workshops for business people, she began cosponsoring in the late 1980s an annual convention, grandly labeled The World Conference of Astro-Economics, which brings together several hundred astrologers interested in business consulting. Lectures, seminars, tapes, and videos are offered for the ever-growing clientele.

Speaking at the third annual conference in 1990 in Chicago was German astrologer and financial adviser Dr. Hans Gerhard Lenz. He devises economic horoscopes for entire countries, which he then uses to make specific predictions for the near future, such as whether the value of the U.S. dollar will go up or the price of oil will go down. Lenz always checks three factors before recommending a stock to his clients: the overall position of the stars, the general horoscope of the market on which the stock is traded, and the astrological prospects of the company selling the stock, which he charts by using the company's "birth date," or date of incorporation. "If these are flowing in the same direction," Lenz says, "then one can say one has a stock that has the potential for greater-than-average growth."

Lenz admits that astro-economics is given less credi-

bility in Europe than in the United States, and he exercises elaborate discretion in dealing with his publicity-shy German clients. Nevertheless, he has become a successful stock market astrologer with a stable of international private and corporate investors who like what he does for them. Business people, according to Lenz and other unconventional financial advisers, are interested in any method that gets results. Comments Arch Crawford, "If I were to take what I have found to the scientific community, they wouldn't want to hear about it. But if I can show results to the Wall Street community, they'll buy it. They don't care what you do. Just come up with the bottom line!"

The bottom line has also long been of paramount interest to Uri Geller, the controversial Israeli clairvoyant and psychokineticist who claims to have been employing paranormal powers since he first bent a soupspoon at age four. Geller has also worked as a psychic consultant to a variety of businesses around the world, though not in the field of astrology. He reports that he has been paid millions of dollars for his consulting work, most of it for advising companies where to look in remote locations for gold, diamonds, oil, and other precious commodities.

Geller's first job at psychic prospecting came during the early 1970s, when he met with the chairman of South Africa's Anglo-Transvaal mining company in his Johannesburg office. There, in front of several highly skeptical geologists, Geller was asked to demonstrate his skills by finding a small piece of gold that the chairman had hidden in the room. Geller quickly located it. "Next they rolled out a huge map on a table, asking me to have a look at it and tell them which was the area with the best coal deposits," he recalled in his 1986 book The Geller Effect. Geller spread his hands above the map and moved them around in the air. "I feel something here," he said, pointing to one specific location. The geologists marked the map. Geller says he never knew if the company actually found coal at the indicated spot until several years later when a Newsweek reporter who was doing a story on him asked the mining company's chairman about the incident. The chairman said that the company

Dowsers divining with forked sticks (below and right, top) are among the essential workers in mining operations pictured in a pair of sixteenth-century German woodcuts. Throughout Europe and in Britain, profitable lodes of gold, silver, copper, lead, tin, and iron were said to have been found by dowsing. Though widely trusted, the practice was then, as now, poorly understood and sometimes denounced as demonic. One seventeenth-century English writer defended the divining rod as a benign instrument, "of Kin to the Load-stone, drawing Iron to it by a secret vertue, inbred by nature, and not by any coniuration as some have fondly imagined."

Virgula diuina

Instrumentum Tractorium

Clayton McDowell, a veteran oil dowser, uses nylon rods to check the ground near a southern Illinois oil rig. He prefers to dowse while driving a Cadillac, with his wife, Marge, helping him steer. This method led McDowell to thirty-three well sites in 1983, thirty of which yielded useful amounts of oil.

Colonel Harry Grattan, a retired British army engineer, shows that his hazel twig does not react to a stream when he is seeking underground water. In 1952, when building a base for British troops occupying Germany, Gratton dowsed an aquifer that still provides a million gallons of water a day.

had indeed discovered large deposits of coal in the precise strip of land that Geller had identified on the map.

Several oil companies, says Geller, have also hired him to help them with explorations. For these assignments, Geller flies over areas chosen by the companies and acts as a human divining rod, pointing out places where he senses oil can be found. Geller will not divulge the names of his oil company clients, claiming they do not wish to be associated with the occult. But he says four of the eleven oil sites he selected for his clients eventually panned out. In another, highly publicized incident, Geller was credited with making possible the building of a $500 million hotel, condominium, and shopping center development near Orlando, Florida. The presidents of the two companies involved, John Aoki of Japan's Aoki Corporation and John Tishman of the United States' Tishman Realty, were hesitant about closing the deal—until Geller predicted that the venture would be a success.

Geller is by no means the only psi practitioner to have put his talents to work for corporate interests. More and more psychics have become corporate specialists. One Los Angeles sensitive, Leslie Lewis, specializes in helping companies solve their security problems. In 1984, the owner of a stereo store in Denver hired Lewis to uncover who among his employees was stealing the store's expensive equipment. Lewis spent hours analyzing handwriting samples from all the store workers. He also studied the store's personnel files, putting together psychic and astrological profiles for each employee. Finally, Lewis drew up descriptions of two suspects, who were eventually apprehended and found responsible for the thefts. The store owner was so pleased with Lewis's work that he hung a large sign in the shop: THIS STORE IS UNDER PSYCHIC SURVEILLANCE.

New York City psychic Shawn Robbins says she worked as a consultant to one of the nation's largest cosmetic companies during the early 1970s. Her job: to use her psychic senses to gauge how the public would respond to new products and new advertising campaigns. "One of my first assignments was to project sales figures for a roll-on deodorant several months in advance," she wrote in her 1980 autobiography. "I had to rely entirely on my psychic gift, for I wasn't even given previous sales figures to go by. Almost instantly a number came to mind. I could see it plainly in my mind's eye, like an event in a dream." Her prediction turned out to be accurate within a few hundred dollars, she said, which immediately won her the respect of even the most skeptical executives in the company.

A few months later, Robbins experienced a strong, uneasy fear while talking to one of the company's vice presidents on the telephone. He had called to tell her not to come into the office that afternoon because he and some associates were flying to a meeting in Denver on a company jet. Acting on her intuition, Robbins warned him not to get on the plane; but the vice president just laughed. "And then I saw it," Robbins recalled. "I saw the serial number on the plane: 297031. At the same time, I 'knew' the pilot's name: Dan Rivers. And I knew if that plane ever got off the ground something terrible would happen."

Robbins described her vision to the executive, but he still would not be talked out of making the trip. An hour later, however, he called her from the airport. "Now it was his turn to be hysterical," Robbins recalled. "The serial number I had given him was an exact hit, except that two of the digits were out of order." And that was not all: The pilot had called in sick that morning and had been replaced by a man named Dan Rivers. At the executive's request, Robbins drove to the airport where she psychically examined the plane. Within minutes, she sensed something was wrong with the left engine. The flight was canceled and the plane examined. Two days later, according to Robbins, the executive called to tell her that mechanics had discovered an improp-

Canadian veterinarian Robert Brewer prepares to use a dowsing rod to pinpoint the infirmity of a champion racehorse. Some adepts have used dowsing to diagnose human ailments and prescribe treatments.

Holding a small pendulum over the sausages, dowser Elizabeth Albright evaluates the freshness of prepackaged meats in a supermarket in Danville, Vermont. Her badge identifies her as a speaker at the annual Danville convention of the American Society of Dowsers.

erly installed replacement pump in the jet's left engine.

Many psychics count individual businesspersons among their regular clients, ranging from well-known fashion designers to behind-the-scenes real-estate developers. In fact, some psychic practitioners claim that business people make up more than 60 percent of their clientele. Those who seek advice are often concerned about whether or not to change jobs or how a business deal will turn out. A Manhattan psychic known by the single name Yolana explains that if a developer wants to sell property, "I may come up with the name of the buyer." Or if a client wants to know what another company is up to, "I'll tell them if there's a merger and what the people involved are like."

Yolana has also consulted with New York fashion designer Diane von Furstenberg, who does not always heed her advice. "She has as much or as little influence as my lawyer or my mother," says Furstenberg. "I'm not sure I would change my mind in respect to something she said, but she is a point of reference and confirmation." Another designer, Christian Dior, was reportedly more attentive to his psychic's readings. He was said to rely on his seer's advice when planning the dates of his fashion showings.

In the world of psychics there are those people who appear to have some special sensitivity to electro- or geomagnetic fields emanating from the earth. These psychics, called dowsers, are adept in an ancient art that has been practiced in many cultures around the world. While dowsing has also been dogged by skepticism and disbelief, many modern businesses admit to hiring dowsers to help in the search for ores, minerals, oil, and other buried riches.

Unlike Uri Geller, who can seemingly locate an area's mineral deposits by simply concentrating on a map, most dowsers survey the prospective site and use divining instruments to locate hidden substances. Some employ a traditional forked willow twig; others use pitchforks, pendulums, or pennies on a wire; still others use only their hands, spreading them wide above the ground as they walk. Usually, the dowser knows he or she has discovered something when the instrument moves, apparently under its own power. "The rod may start to leap about as though some unseen hand is trying to wrestle it away, only to return to quiescence as soon as the dowser seems to get out of range," wrote one observer.

Skeptics claim that dowsers are no better at locating gold veins or productive oil wells than anyone else making random guesses at the same sites. Nevertheless, dowsers have been credited with some remarkable successes, especially in the oil business. Indeed, some of the most productive oil fields in the United States are said to have been discovered by dowsers. In the early 1940s, for example, J. W. Young, a farmer from Edmond, Oklahoma, took his dowsing instrument—a goatskin-covered bottle hanging from a watch chain—and tested it over a piece of town property. The bottle swung north to south, just as it had done during earlier trials when Young had held it over oil. This was enough evidence to convince Young and, eventually, wildcatter Ace Gutowski that oil lay beneath Edmond's parched soil. In 1943, Gutowski drilled where Young had dowsed—and promptly hit the largest oil field discovered in Oklahoma since the oil heyday of the 1920s.

Paul Clement Brown, a graduate of the Massachusetts Institute of Technology and a former electronic engineer, began dowsing for oil during the 1950s. He had become curious about the ancient practice after watching a group of dowsers prospecting for oil near where he had been searching with more conventional electronic methods. Brown soon found that he had a knack for dowsing. In fact, he became so good at it that he claimed to be able to predict the amount of oil a well would produce.

During his first job for J. K. Wadley, one of the industry's most successful wildcatters, Brown predicted that oil lay precisely 2,700 feet down at a particular site, and that a well drilled there would bring in about 150 barrels a day. Although two nearby sites had earlier come up empty, Wadley decided—acting on his own hunch about the psychic—to

ORIGINAL COMPOSITE MASTER MAP

go ahead and drill where Brown suggested. Two weeks later, he called Brown into his office. "Your prediction was pretty good," Wadley said, in a wry tone. "That Cascade well struck oil at 2,700 feet and it's making 150 barrels a day. We drilled three more wells into the trend and they're each producing 150 barrels as well." Wadley signed Brown to a contract and relied on his dowsing advice for years.

Brown dowsed with a petroleum-filled cylinder dangling on a string. He also carried a special stopwatch, whose face he had changed to show feet of depth. With these two simple tools, he said, he could determine precise information about a potential oil well. "I press the button on the top of the watch, starting it from zero, and hold my pendulum steady and motionless," he explained. "The watch reads off ninety feet of depth every minute. At one point, when the watch has recorded a given depth, say 5,000 feet, the pendulum will start swinging in a circle counterclockwise, at which point I will say, 'In.' That depth indicates the top surface of a bed of oil-producing sand. The pendulum will continue to rotate counterclockwise until the watch hand reads 5,120 feet, whereupon it will stop. At that point I say, 'Out.' I have reached the bottom of the oil production zone and know it is 120 feet thick."

To determine how much oil a well would produce from a particular zone, Brown measured the intensity of the pendulum's twirling motion. Then, after considering all his findings, he would assign each potential well site to one of four categories: "not commercially productive," "good," "very good," or "excellent."

Brown dowsed for minerals as well as for oil and gas. While working in California's San Bernardino Mountains, he and his petroleum-filled pendulum located the first deposit of a rare platinum-bearing ore called laurelite ever found in the United States. He also stumbled upon a large uranium find while checking out an oil site for Wadley. "He sent me up to the Ambrosia Lake area near Grants, New Mexico, where he had drilled an expensive dry hole," Brown remembered. "He wanted me to determine if the rest of the area was devoid of oil. So I went up there and I found the reason why they weren't finding any oil was because there wasn't any oil up there. I came back and told Wadley: 'Chief, there's no place to drill for oil up there but your lease covers the finest deposit of uranium I've ever seen. You should go for that since the same lease allows for the development of both oil and minerals.'"

Wadley carefully considered what Brown told him but after a few days decided to go against his dowser's advice and quitclaim the land back to its owners. He made the wrong choice. "A short while later it produced six million dollars' worth of uranium for its owners," Brown said. "He'd walked away from six million just like that!"

In 1945 the late J. B. Rhine, a guru of psychic investigation, wrote that no practical use could be made of ESP and psychokinesis with our present state of knowledge; "They are not reliable enough," he concluded. The day may be closer now when that prediction will be reversed. We live in a time when trends come and go almost overnight, an age in which, as CAI founder William Kautz puts it, "basic human change takes only one generation to occur." In this fast-moving age of communication a flood of knowledge threatens to swamp executive decisions. Computers can process this information with amazing speed, but as professor and intuition researcher Weston Agor points out, "computer projections for the future have never been terribly reliable, even in the most stable of times, as a basis for making decisions. They are likely to become less so in the future."

Thus, for Agor, Kautz, and many others involved in psychic research, the need for a new way of approaching the decision-making process is crucial for the success of a business—perhaps of any enterprise. For these observers, a greater reliance on intuition and other psychic tools is clearly part of the answer. "There is now a premium on managers with precognition," says Agor, "the psychic ability to see the future." As intuition expert Roy Rowan puts it, "Logic and analysis can lead a person only partway down the path to a profitable decision. The last step to success frequently requires a daring intuitive leap."

Mind over Matter

In high-tech research facilities around the world, certain individuals gain a reputation as laboratory jinxes; their very presence inexplicably causes complex equipment to malfunction in bizarre ways. Psychic investigators have long suspected that this suggests a human-and-machine interaction on an unseen level. To Dean Radin *(above)*, a researcher at AT&T's Bell Labs, it presented an even more intriguing possibility—that perhaps machines could be controlled by the mind.

In 1981, Radin set out to investigate how psychokinetic power could be brought to bear deliberately on a computer system. In 1990, building upon earlier research at Bell Labs and at Princeton University, he began experiments using a commercial integrated circuit called the AT&T T7001, a random number generator (RNG) on a microchip. The T7001 produces a stream of random bits— unordered on-off signals that amount to electronic noise in which no pattern can be predicted or discerned.

Radin asked subjects to concentrate for ten-second intervals on the chip as it operated. Computer analysis showed that the sequence of bits generated during each ten-second period created a pattern that differed from the random noise otherwise produced by the chip. These results, said Radin, supported his hypothesis that at least "in principle, some computer failures may be psi-mediated." Moreover, they suggested a promising avenue to follow in creating psi-controlled machines. By combining RNGs with computerized pattern recognition and robotic technology, human thought might be used to operate security and communication systems—maybe even to enable paraplegics to will their lifeless limbs into action.

Patterns that Send a Message

When human thought affects the electronic noise produced by a random number generator, the result is a pattern impressed upon the noise. Converted to numbers and plotted on a graph, the pattern becomes an identifiable configuration that Dean Radin calls a mind print. Because a mind print, like a fingerprint, is unique to an individual, a computer can be programmed to recognize and employ it in security systems that bar entrance to all but authorized persons.

Illustrated in principle here, the technological tools for the task make up a hypothetical device Radin believes might some day be possible. Thinking "open the door," the operator *(below left)* affects the signals generated by an RNG, represented here by the chip next to the operator. The result is a sequence of numbers that are read by a neural network (represented by the chips at right below), a type of computer software particularly adept at recognizing patterns. The network recognizes the pattern as a mind print *(below),* matches it with a previously stored print, and sends a signal to open the door. In theory, a neural network could identify and store the mind prints that express a given mental intention—such as "open the door"—for any authorized operator.

4   10   6   5   8

Because psychokinesis is thought to operate independently of constraints imposed by distance or physical barriers, a psi telecommunications system might conceivably be used in areas where electromagnetic signals cannot penetrate, such as under water or in deep mines. Here, an onshore operator is hooked up to monitoring equipment that informs him (via the computer screen in front of him) when his nervous system and local environmental conditions are in the optimal mode to send a mental message to the RNG and neural network aboard a submerged submarine. The transmission, in the form of a mind print that matches a previously recorded print in the on-board neural network, might signal the sub to surface or change course.

Controlling Limbs with Computerized Thought

A quadriplegic, whose biological links between brain and muscle have been severed by accident or illness, is here fitted with a lightweight metal exoskeleton wired to a bank of RNGs and tiny neural networks stored in a backpack. Each joint in his hands and arms is controlled by one of the little computers that stores a series of mind prints, each representing an instruction to move that joint in a predetermined fashion. Thus, the man's mental intention to raise his arm, picked up by the RNGs and interpreted by the neural networks, sends the signals that instruct servomotors to move the otherwise immobile joints. If perfected, similar devices could be used to control an independent robot by thought.

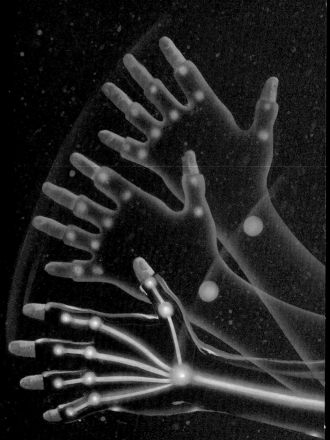

ACKNOWLEDGMENTS

The editors wish to thank the following individuals and institutions for their valuable assistance in the preparation of this volume:

Camillo Albertini, Rizzoli, Milan, Italy; Bill Aldrich, Chicago; Malcolm Bessent, Surbiton, Surrey, England; Giovanni Canonico, Edizioni Mediterranee, Rome; Donald G. Cherry, Hyattsville, Maryland; Nicola Cutolo, Bari, Italy; Lt. Daniel Davis, Ellicott City, Maryland; Dr. Baldur R. Ebertin, Bad Wildbad, Germany; Al Hardin, Pentagon Library, Washington, D.C.; Alexander Imich, New York; Beverly Jaegers, Sappington, Maryland; Joyce LaJudice, Lily Dale Assembly, Lily Dale, New York; Sandra Martin, New York; Jim Merrithew, Lanark, Ontario, Canada; Dean Radin, Waltham, Massachusetts; Volker Schumacher, Institut für Grenzgebiete der Psychologie und Psychohygiene, Freiburg, Germany; Anita Smith, Scottsdale, Arizona; Ingo Swann, New York; Marian Swida, Chicago.

PICTURE CREDITS

The sources for the illustrations in this book are listed below. Credits from left to right are separated by semicolons; credits from top to bottom are separated by dashes.

Cover: Art by Greg Harlin of Stansbury, Ronsaville and Wood, Inc. 7: Michael Laughlin, © The Chicago Tribune/Sygma (detail from page 16). 8, 9: *Dallas Morning News,* November 23, 1963—Abraham Zapruder; Steve Schapiro for *Life.* 10, 11: Bill Ray for *Life—Anchorage Daily Times,* March 29, 1964. 12, 13: British Library, London—Bill Ray for *Life;* Miroslav Kucera, Chocen, Czechoslovakia. 14, 15: Courtesy Alan Vaughan, Los Angeles; UPI/Bettmann, New York—*Evening Times,* Trenton, New Jersey, June 23, 1972. 16: *Chicago Tribune,* May 26, 1979—Michael Laughlin, © The Chicago Tribune/Sygma. 17: Michael Laughlin, © The Chicago Tribune/Sygma; AP/Wide World Photos, New York. 18, 19: AP/Wide World Photos, New York; © Keith and Dorothy Stoffel, Spokane, Washington—*Daily Olympian,* Olympia, Washington, May 19, 1980. 20, 21: *St. Louis Business Journal;* AP/Wide World Photos, New York; © 1986 The New York Times Company. Reprinted by permission. 22, 23: Eric Bouvet/Gamma-Liaison, New York; Henry Groskinsky—*Washington Post,* November 10, 1989; Berliner Morgenpost Ullstein Verlag, Berlin. 25: Art by Time-Life Books based on a photograph courtesy of AP/Wide World Photos, New York. 26: Private collection. 28, 29: Lily Dale Assembly, Lily Dale, New York; Fortean Picture Library, Clwyd, Wales. 30, 31: Mary Evans Picture Library, London; Public Record Office, London (MEPO 3/142)—Mary Evans Picture Library, London. 32: Mander and Mitchenson Theatre Collection, Beckenham, Kent—The Hulton Picture Company, London. 33: Harry Price Collection/Mary Evans Picture Library, London. 35: UPI/Bettman, New York. 36: Popperfoto, Overstone, Northamptonshire. 39: Natal Newspapers, Durban, South Africa. 40: Time-Life Books; courtesy Howard County Police Department, Maryland, from *FBI Law Enforcement Bulletin,* August 1977. 41: Courtesy Howard County Police Department, Maryland, from *FBI Law Enforcement Bulletin,* August 1977, drawing by Donald "Gideon" Cherry; courtesy Howard County Police Department, Maryland, from *FBI Law Enforcement Bulletin,* August 1977. 42: Courtesy Irene F. Hughes, Chicago; Canapress Photo Service, Toronto (4). 45: AP/Wide World Photos, New York—Alex Antoniades, Nutley, New Jersey. 46: Al Petschonek, Charlack, Missouri. 47: Vincent J. Musi, Pittsburgh. 49: Art by Bryan Leister (detail from page 54). 50-57: Art by Bryan Leister. 58, 59: Bundesarchiv, Koblenz, Germany; from *Astrologische Familien-Chronik* by Elsbeth Ebertin, Dreizack-Verlag, Hamburg, 1931; from *Ein Blick in die Zukunft* by Elsbeth Ebertin, published by Fr. Paul Lorenz, 1923. 60, 61: Ullstein Bilderdienst, Berlin; Bildarchiv Preussischer Kulturbesitz, Berlin; Ullstein Bilderdienst, Berlin (2)—Keystone Pressedienst, Hamburg. 62, 63: Ullstein Bilderdienst, Berlin; Collection Ellic Howe, London; Barnaby's Picture Library, London—Gianni Dagli Orti, Paris—Collection Ellic Howe, London. 64, 65: Wewelsburg Museum, Wewelsburg, Germany; National Archives; Süddeutscher Verlag Bilderdienst, Munich—Mario Fenyo, courtesy National Archives. 66, 67: Courtesy Dora Isakovna; Library of Congress—CAF, Warsaw. 68, 69: The Hulton Picture Company, London; Süddeutscher Verlag Bilderdienst, Munich; Imperial War Museum, London; Werner Schüring, courtesy Institut für Grenzgebiete der Psychologie und Psychohygiene, Freiburg; The Hulton Picture Company, London—U.S. Coast Guard, National Archives, neg. no. 26-G-1514. 71: Art by Time-Life Books based on a photograph courtesy of Ullstein Bilderdienst, Berlin. 72, 73: Archives Tallandier, Paris. 74: Culver Pictures, New York. 75: Roger-Viollet, Paris. 76: © 1984 Ronald M. McRae, from the book *Mind Wars* and reprinted with permission from St. Martin's Press, Inc., New York. 77: Montana Historical Society, Helena. 78: Louis Matacia; courtesy the United States Marine Corps, from *The Divining Hand* by Christopher Bird, E. P. Dutton, New York, 1979. 80: From archive of Edward K. Naumov, Moscow. 81: Jaroslav Kulhavy, Vseradice, Czechoslovakia. 85: Henry Groskinsky. 86: H. E. Puthoff, Ph.D., Austin, Texas. 87: Dario Coletti, Daylight, Rome. 88: Robert G. Jahn, from *Margins of Reality* by Robert G. Jahn and Brenda J. Dunne, Harcourt Brace Jovanovich, 1988. 89: Courtesy The Mobius Society, Los Angeles—© 1981 The Mobius Society, Los Angeles. 90: PSI TECH, Albuquerque, New Mexico. 92, 93: Fabian/Sygma, New York; D-Day, Padua, Italy. 95: Topham Picture Source, Edenbridge, Kent (detail from page 100). 96, 97: Nicola Cutolo, Bari, from *L'Energia che guarisce* by Nicola Cutolo, published by Edizioni Mediterranee, 1985, Rome; Roger-Viollet, Paris; Jean-Loup Charmet, Paris. 98, 99: Topham Picture Source, New York; © 1990 Dilip Mehta/Contact Press Images, New York. 100: Topham Picture Source, Edenbridge, Kent. 101: Dr. Elmar R. Gruber/Fortean Picture Library, Clwyd, Wales—Silvano Bergamaschi/"Oggi," Milan. 102: Gert Chesi, from *Faith Healers in the Philippines* by Gert Chesi, Perlinger Verlag, Wörgl, Austria, 1981. 103: Sergei Mikhailovich Kuznetzov, Moscow, 1988; Topham Picture Source, Edenbridge, Kent. 105: Time-Life Books. 106: Philippe Halsman/© 1967 Yvonne Halsman. 108, 109: John Harding, San Francisco. 110: UPI/Bettmann, New York. 111: Henry Groskinsky. 112: Thomas S. England. 114: Bill Sperry. 116: Darlene Moore, San Francisco (2); drawing by Keith Harary, Ph.D., San Francisco. 117: Drawings by Keith Harary, Ph.D., San Francisco. 118, 119: Grace K. Morris. 120, 121: AP/Wide World Photos, New York; Finanzen Verlagsgesellschaft, Munich. 122, 123: Shipi Shtrang, Berkshire; courtesy Uri Geller, Berkshire. 125: Jean-Loup Charmet, Paris. 126, 127: John Beckett, London. 129: © 1987 Seaview Exploration Associates. 131: Courtesy Dean I. Radin, Waltham, Massachusetts. 132-137: Art by Will Willams of Stansbury, Ronsaville and Wood, Inc.

BIBLIOGRAPHY

Agor, Weston H.:
   "All about Intuition." *Boardroom Reports,* December 15, 1991.
   Intuitive Management. Englewood Cliffs, N.J.: Prentice-Hall, 1984.
   "The Logic of Intuition: How Top Executives Make Important Decisions." *Organizational Dynamics,* 1986.
Alexander, John B., "The New Mental Battlefield: 'Beam Me Up, Spock.'" *Military Review,* December 1980.
Alexander, John B., Richard Groller, and Janet Morris, *The Warrior's Edge.* New York: William Morrow, 1990.
Alphier, James E., and Thomas D. Williams, "W. D. Gann: The 'Mystic.'" *Commodities Magazine,* May 1982.
Barrett, William, and Theodore Besterman, *The Divining Rod.* Toronto: Coles, 1979.

Bartlett, Kay, "Future Is Clear to Psychic Robbins, and She'll Gladly Tell It—For a Fee." *Los Angeles Times,* February 28, 1988.
Bartlett, Laile E., *Psi Trek.* New York: McGraw-Hill, 1981.
Berger, Arthur S., and Joyce Berger, *The Encyclopedia of Parapsychology and Psychical Research.* New York: Paragon House, 1991.
Billington, James H., "Czechoslovakia Resists." *Life,* September 6, 1968.
Bird, Christopher:
   The Divining Hand. New York: E. P. Dutton, 1979.
   "The Making of an Oil Dowser, Part III." *Fate,* May 1988.
Block, Barbara, "Intuition Creeps Out of the Closet and into the Boardroom." *Management Review,* May 1990.
Britz, Ellen, "The Sixth Sense." *Entrepreneurial Woman,* March 1991.

Broughton, Richard S., *Parapsychology: The Controversial Science.* New York: Ballantine Books, 1991.
Brown, Raymond Lamont, *Phantom Soldiers.* New York: Drake, 1975.
Channon, Jim, *Evolutionary Tactics.* Washington, D.C.: The First Earth Battalion, 1982.
Church, George J., "Freedom!" *Time,* November 20, 1989.
Cook, James, "Closing the Psychic Gap." *Forbes,* May 21, 1984.
Crawford, Arch:
   "Good Times and Bad Times, a Potpourri." *Crawford Perspectives,* June 29, 1991.
   "No Sign of a Bottom!" *Crawford Perspectives,* October 10, 1987.

Crowley, Lyle, "Prophets of Profit." *Manhattan, Inc.,* January 1990.

Crudele, John, "Market Cyclists Predict Dow Going Much Lower." *New York Post,* July 27, 1990.

"A DC-10 Crashes near Chicago in the Worst U.S. Air Disaster." *Time,* June 4, 1979.

De Wohl, Louis, *I Follow My Stars.* London: George G. Harrap, 1937.

Deacon, Richard:
  The Truth Twisters. London: Macdonald, 1987.
  With My Little Eye: The Memoirs of a Spy Hunter. London: Frederick Muller, 1982.

Dean, Douglas, et al., *Executive ESP.* Englewood Cliffs, N.J.: Prentice-Hall, 1974.

Dean, Douglas, and John Mihalasky, "Testing for Executive ESP." *Psychic,* November-December 1974.

Decker, Robert, and Barbara Decker, "The Eruptions of Mount St. Helens." *Scientific American,* March 1981.

Delmer, Sefton, *Black Boomerang.* New York: Viking Press, 1962.

"Doomsday Headaches." *Science Digest,* February 1982.

Doyle, Arthur Conan, *Letters to the Press.* Iowa City: University of Iowa Press, 1986.

"Dream Murder." Transcript from 20/20 television news show no. 730. New York: ABC News, August 6, 1987.

Druckman, Daniel, and John A. Swets, eds., *Enhancing Human Performance.* Washington, D.C.: National Academy Press, 1988.

Druffel, Ann:
  "The Psychic Laboratory of the Mobius Society." *Fate,* June 1989.
  "The Psychic Laboratory of the Mobius Society Part 2." *Fate,* July 1989.

Dubin, Susan Schraub, "Stocks and the Stars: Profiting from the Planets." *Harper's Bazaar,* October 1985.

Ebon, Martin:
  Prophecy in Our Time. New York: New American Library, 1968.
  Psychic Warfare: Threat or Illusion? New York: McGraw-Hill, 1983.

Edgerton, Jerry, Junius Ellis, and Jordan E. Goodman, "What the Heavens Say: Sell by Mid-July When Jupiter Exits Taurus." *Money,* June 1988.

Emerson, Steven, *Secret Warriors: Inside the Covert Military Operations of the Reagan Era.* New York: G. P. Putnam's Sons, 1988.

Fairley, John, and Simon Welfare, *Arthur C. Clarke's World of Strange Powers.* London: Collins, 1984.

Fisher, Joe, *Predictions.* New York: Van Nostrand Reinhold, 1980.

"Four Days That Stopped America." *Life,* November 1983.

Frazier, Kendrick. "Bent Spoons Turn to Gold for Uri Geller." *Skeptical Inquirer,* Winter 1986-1987.

Geller, Uri, and Guy Lyon Playfair, *The Geller Effect.* London: Jonathan Cape, 1986.

Gilardi, John, "Looking for Stellar Stock Performance? So Are They." *Business,* November 2, 1990.

Gittelson, Bernard, and Laura Torbet, *Intangible Evidence.* New York: Simon & Schuster, 1987.

Great Disasters. Pleasantville, N.Y.: Reader's Digest Association, 1989.

Gunther, Max, *Wall Street and Witchcraft.* New York: Bernard Geis, 1971.

Hibbard, Whitney S., *Psychic Criminology.* Springfield, Ill.: Charles C. Thomas, 1982.

Hannula, Hans, "Ganntrader 2" (product review). *Stocks & Commodities,* September 1991.

Honegger, Barbara, and Jeffrey Mishlove, "Security Implications of Applied Psi: An Historical Summary." *Applied Psi Newsletter,* November-December 1982.

Howard, Jane, "Jeane Dixon's Prophecies." *Life,* October 8, 1965.

Howe, Ellic:
  Astrology and the Third Reich. Wellingborough, Northamptonshire, England: Aquarian Press, 1984.
  The Black Game. London: Michael Joseph, 1982.

"The Hunch Bunch." *Manchester Guardian,* April 22, 1987.

Hurley, Dan, "The Hit Parade." *Psychology Today,* July 1986.

Hyams, Ron, "Is There Anybody Out There?" *The Unexplained* (London), Vol. 2, Issue 13.

"Intuition and the Stock Market." *Applied Psi* (San Francisco), Fall 1984.

Jackson, Gerald, *Executive ESP.* New York: Pocket Books, 1989.

Jaegers, Beverly C., "Dowser Wins the Gold." *Fate,* October 1986.

Jones, Billy, "W. D. Gann: The Man." *Commodities Magazine,* May 1982.

Kaufman, Joanne:
  "Spellbound." *Savvy,* April 1987.
  "What's New in Parapsychology." *New York Times,* November 3, 1985.

Kautz, William H., and Melanie Branon, *Intuiting the Future.* New York: Harper & Row, 1989.

King, Janine. "Hocus Pocus and High Finance Cut a Deal." *Elle,* August 1991.

King, Patricia, "The Stargazers Strike Back." *Newsweek,* January 15, 1990.

"Larry Pesavento: The Wave Trader." *Wall Street Computer Review,* no date.

Lewis, Jack, "ESP Wins in Las Vegas." *Fate,* October 1987.

Life: The Year in Pictures 1972, December 29, 1972.

Linedecker, Clifford L., *Psychic Spy.* Garden City, N.Y.: Doubleday, 1976.

Lochner, Louis P., transl. and ed., *The Goebbels Diaries.* London: Hamish Hamilton, 1948.

Love, John F., *McDonald's: Behind the Arches.* Toronto: Bantam Books, 1986.

Lungin, Tatiana, *Wolf Messing: The True Story of Russia's Greatest Psychic.* Transl. by Cynthia Rosenberger and John Glad. Ed. by D. Scott Rogo. New York: Paragon House, 1989.

Lyons, Arthur, and Marcello Truzzi, *The Blue Sense: Psychic Detectives and Crime.* New York: The Mysterious Press, 1991.

McRae, Ronald M., *Mind Wars: The True Story of Government Research into the Military Potential of Psychic Weapons.* New York: St. Martin's Press, 1984.

Malone, Roy, "Coffee Fortune Laid to Brazil Freeze, ESP." *St. Louis Post-Dispatch,* May 20, 1976.

Marcial, Gene G., and Jeffrey M. Laderman, "Hits and Misses: Who Saw the Stampede Coming." *Business Week,* February 18, 1985.

"Modern Mystics." *Elle,* August 1991.

"Military Agenda for NASA." *U.S. News & World Report,* June 16, 1986.

Montgomery, Ruth:
  Aliens Among Us. New York: G. P. Putnam's Sons, 1985.
  A Gift of Prophecy: The Phenomenal Jeane Dixon. New York: Bantam Books, 1966.

Morris, Grace. "Working with Businesses." *NCGR Journal,* Spring 1985.

Murdoch, Derrick, *The Agatha Christie Mystery.* Toronto: Pagurian Press, 1976.

The New Order (The Third Reich series). Alexandria, Va.: Time-Life Books, 1989.

Orr, Kathy, "Their Opinion? Look to the Skies." *Southtown Economist,* November 4, 1990.

Patterson, Mary Jo, "The Extrasensory Detective." *Police Magazine,* March 1981.

Pitt, Barrie, and the Editors of Time-Life Books, *The Battle of the Atlantic* (World War II series). Alexandria, Va.: Time-Life Books, 1980.

Psi Research (San Francisco), September-December 1985.

Puthoff, Harold E., and Russell Targ, "A Perceptual Channel for Information Transfer over Kilometer Distances: Historical Perspective and Recent Research." *Proceedings of the IEEE,* March 1976.

Redeffer, Linda, "Bevy Jaegers—The Future is Hers to See." *The Times West,* March 4-11, 1981.

Rhea, Kathlyn, and Maggie O'Leary, *The Psychic Is You.* Millbrae, Calif.: Celestial Arts, 1979.

Rhea, Kathlyn, and Josef Quattro, *Mind Sense.* Berkeley, Calif.: Celestial Arts, 1988.

Rhine, J. B., "Location of Hidden Objects by a Man-Dog Team." *The Journal of Parapsychology,* Vol. 35, 1971.

Robbins, Shawn, as told to Milton Pierce, *Ahead of Myself: Confessions of a Professional Psychic.* Englewood Cliffs, N.J.: Prentice-Hall, 1980.

Roberts, Henry C., transl. and ed., *The Complete Prophecies of Nostradamus.* Ed. by Lee Roberts Amsterdam and Harvey Amsterdam. Oyster Bay, N.Y.: Nostradamus, 1982 (reprint of 1947 edition).

Rogo, D. Scott:
  "ESP at the Races." *Fate,* September 1986.
  Psychic Breakthroughs Today. Wellingborough, Northamptonshire, England: Aquarian Press, 1987.
  "Psychics Beat the Stock Market." *Fate,* July 1984.

Rosenfeld, Albert, "Earthquake in Alaska." *Life,* April 10, 1964.

Rossman, Michael, *New Age Blues.* New York: E. P. Dutton, 1979.

Rowan, Roy, *The Intuitive Manager.* Boston: Little, Brown, 1986.

Rudley, Stephen, *Psychic Detectives.* New York: Franklin Watts, 1979.

"Russians Go Home!" *Time,* August 30, 1968.

Sargent, Carl L., *Exploring Psi in the Ganzfeld.* New York: Parapsychology Foundation, 1980.

Shepard, Leslie A., ed., *Encyclopedia of Occultism & Parapsychology.* Detroit: Gale Research, 1985.

Sklar, Dusty, *Gods and Beasts: The Nazis and the Occult.* New York: Thomas Y. Crowell, 1977.

The SS (The Third Reich series). Alexandria, Va.: Time-Life Books, 1988.

Standard & Poors, *Standard NYSE Stock Reports,* Vol. 581, no. 224, sec. 22, November 20, 1991.

Steiger, Brad, *The Psychic Feats of Olof Jonsson.* Englewood Cliffs, N.J.: Prentice-Hall, 1971.

Stern, Hersh L., "Parapsychology in Business: Some Likely Applications." *Business & Economic Dimensions,* March-April 1976.

Sullivan, Deidre, "The Japanese Dig William Kautz." *World Trade,* May 1991.

Tabori, Paul, *Crime and the Occult.* London: David & Charles, 1974.

Targ, Russell, and Keith Harary, *The Mind Race.* New York: Villard Books, 1984.

Tart, Charles T., *Learning to Use Extrasensory Perception.* Chicago: University of Chicago Press, 1976.

Tobias, Fritz, *The Reichstag Fire*. Transl. by Arnold J. Pomerans. New York: G. P. Putnam's Sons, 1964.

Tuz, Peter:

"Bevy Jaegers' Psychic Picks Baffle the Experts, but Fare Well." *Business Journal*, February 8-14, 1982.

"Jaegers' Stocks up 17 Percent. Is She Psychic? Or Is She Lucky?" *St. Louis Business Journal*, July 12-18, 1982.

"Uri Geller." *The Skeptical Inquirer*, Winter 1986-87.

Varenchik, Richard, "L.A. Court Vindicates Psychic Vision." *Fate*, August 1987.

Vaughan, Alan:

"The Coming Psi Technology." *Applied Psi Newsletter*, November-December 1982.

The Edge of Tomorrow. New York: Coward, McCann & Geoghegan, 1982.

The Power of Positive Prophecy. London: Aquarian Press, 1991.

Walther, Herbert, ed., *Hitler*. New York: Exeter Books, 1978.

White, John, ed., *Psychic Warfare: Fact or Fiction?* Wellingborough, Northamptonshire, England: Aquarian Press, 1988.

Wilcox, Tamara, *Mysterious Detectives: Psychics*. Milwaukee: Raintree Childrens Books, 1977.

Wilhelm, John L., *The Search for Superman*. New York: Pocket Books, 1976.

Wilson, Colin, *The Psychic Detectives*. San Francisco: Mercury House, 1985.

Woodward, Kenneth L., "The Strange Visions of Dorothy Allison." *McCall's*, September 1978.

The World Almanac and Book of Facts 1990. New York: World Almanac, 1990.

Wulff, Wilhelm, *Zodiac and Swastika*. New York: Coward, McCann & Geoghegan, 1973.

Yeterian, Dixie, *Casebook of a Psychic Detective*. New York: Stein and Day, 1982.

Index

Numerals in italics indicate an illustration of the subject mentioned.

A

Abbott, David P., 34

Adams, Evangeline, 120-121

Aetherius Society, *100*

Agnes, Hurricane, *14-15*

Agor, Weston: and executive ESP, 107, 130; and precognition, 130; quoted, 107, 130; and Frances E. Vaughan, 107

Ahead of Myself (Robbins), 113, 127

Aken, Myrna Joy, *39;* disappearance and murder of, 35-36, 39; and Nelson Palmer, 35-36, 37, 39; and Clarence Van Buuren, 36-37, 39

Alaska, *10-11*

Albright, Elizabeth, *127*

Alexander, Greta, *26;* and Mary Cousett, 24, 25-27; and William Fitzgerald, 24, 25, 27; and lightning, 25, 26; and psychic detection, 24-27; quoted, 25, 26; and spirits, 26; and Steve Trew, 26

Alexander, John B., 90-91

Allison, Dorothy, 43-*45*

Anderson, Jack, 80

Anderson, William, 71

Angel, J. Lawrence, 40

Ankrah, Joseph A., 76

Anschluss, 64

Aoki, John, 126

Apollo I (spacecraft), 41

Applied cybernetics, 80

Art of War, The (Sun Tzu), 73

Astro-economics: and Arch Crawford, 121-123, 124; and eclipses, 123; and Robert Hand, 121; and Hans Gerhard Lenz, 121, 124; and Grace Morris, 118-119, 123-124; and stock market, 118

Astrolabe, 121

"Astrologie und Okkultismus" (radio broadcast), 68

Astrology: and Beatrice Foods, *118-119;* and Napoleon Bonaparte, *75;* and Central Intelligence Agency, 76; criticism of, 65; and John Dee, 74; and Walt Disney, 111; and W. D. Gann, 118; and Rudolf Hess, 64, 65; and Heinrich Himmler, 64, 65; and Adolf Hitler, 64; and Hans Gerhard Lenz, 124; pamphlets about, *69;*

and Robert Mandlestam, 76; and J. P. Morgan, 120-121; and Grace Morris, 118-119, 123-124; natal charts of, *118-119;* and Nazis, *69;* and Kwame Nkrumah, 76; and psychic detection, 27; and Ronald Reagan, 91; and stock market, *118-119,* 120; and Achmed Sukarno, 76-77; and David Williams, 119

Astro-Market Letter (journal), 121

Astronomy, 118

Atlanta child murders, 44; and Dorothy Allison, 43, 44; and Wayne Williams, 44

Auras, 113

Ayurveda, 98

Ayurvedic Institute, 98-99

B

Bach, Richard: and SCANATE, 81; and *Taurus*, 83

Ball, Joseph A., 82

Beacons, 85

Beatrice Foods, natal charts of, *118-119*

Beer Hall Putsch: and Adolf Hitler, 58, 62, *63;* and Nazis, 58

Bergier, Jacques: death of, 71; and Gérald Messadié, 71; and *Nautilus*, 71, 72; and psi-warfare experiments, 72

Berlin Wall, *22-23*

Bessent, Malcolm, *111*

Bible: and W. D. Gann, 118; psi-warfare experiments in, 73; psychic detection in, 27

Bio Chromo-Relax Institute, *101*

Biophysics Laboratory, 84

Biowork, 94

Black Tuesday, 112. *See also* Stock market crash (1929)

Blue bottles, *30-31*

Bodywork, 94

Bonaparte, Napoleon, *75*

Booth, David, *17*

Bowers, William, 71

Brejack, George, 44

Brewer, Robert, *127*

Bridger, Jim, *77*

Brighton trunk crime, and Eugenie Dennis, 34, *36*

Britain, and psi-warfare experiments, *68-69*

Broughton, Richard, 94

Brown, Paul Clement, 128-130

Buchanan, Joseph Rodes (*Manual of Psychometry*), 30

C

CAI. *See* Center for Applied Intuition

Carrington, Hereward, 34

Catchings, John, *52-53;* and lightning, 49; and Gail Lorke, *49-57;* and Ronald Phillips, 56; and psychic detection, *49-57;* quoted, 49, 55; and Ronald Roark, 49; and Marty Wing, 53, 56

Center for Applied Intuition (CAI): and William Kautz, *108,* 109, 130; purposes of, 109

Central Intelligence Agency (CIA): and Joseph A. Ankrah, 76; and astrology, 76; and clairvoyance, 80, 81; and Miles Copeland, 76; and ESP, 85; and Robert Mandlestam, 76; and Kwame Nkrumah, 76; and parapsychology, 80, 91; and psi-warfare experiments, 76, 79, 80, 81-82; and Harold Puthoff, 81; and SCANATE, 81-82; and SRI International, 81-82, 83, 85; and Achmed Sukarno, 76-77; and Ingo Swann, 85; and Russell Targ, 81

Challenger (space shuttle), *20-21*

Channon, Jim, 94

Cherry, Donald, drawings by, *40-41*

Christie, Agatha, *32;* disappearance of, 29, 32; and Arthur Conan Doyle, 29, 32; and Scotland Yard, 29

Chromotherapy, *101*

Church, George W., 81

Church of Scientology, 84

Clairvoyance: and Central Intelligence Agency, 80, 81; defined, 7, 25, 80; and Uri Geller, 124; and Heinrich Himmler, 65; and J. P. Morgan, 111; and psi-warfare experiments, 7; and Harold Puthoff, 80; and SRI International, 80; and Russell Targ, 80, 81; and Cornelius Vanderbilt, 111. *See also* Intuition

"Clairvoyance, Hypnotism, and Magnetic Healing" (Hejbalik), 74

Columbia (space shuttle), 20

Computers: and mind prints, 132; and psi powers, 131; and psychokinesis, 131; and Dean Radin, 131

Brown, Paul Clement, 128-130

Connor, Patrick, 77

Consciousness, 109

Control Data, 116-117

Copeland, Miles (*The Game Player*), 76

Cosmic fishing. *See* Intuition

Cousett, Mary: and Greta Alexander, 24, 25-27; and William Fitzgerald, 24, 25; and Stanley Holliday, Jr., 24, 26-27; murder of, 24

Crawford, Arch, 121-123, *124*

"Crawford Perspectives" (telephone hotline), 121

Croesus (king of Lydia), 74

Cross, James Jasper, 41-43

Crystal balls: and John Dee, 74; and Jeane Dixon, *9;* and psychic detection, 27; purposes of, 74

Cummings, Robert, 41-43

Cunning men. *See* Psychics

Cutolo, Nicola, *96-97, 101*

Cybernetics, applied, 80

Czetli, Nancy, 45-47

D

Daguerreotypes, 30

Dames, Edward, 90

Davitashvili, Djuna, *103*

Dean, Douglas: and executive ESP, 107; and John Mihalasky, *106;* and plethysmograph, *106;* and precognition, 107; and telepathy, 106

Dee, John: and astrology, 74; code name of, *76;* and crystal balls, 74; and Elizabeth I, 74; and "the nine," 74; and psi-warfare experiments, 74

Delmer, Denis Sefton, *68*

Delphi Associates: disbanding of, 117; and Keith Harary, 113, 116; purposes of, 113; and stock market, 113, 115, 116-117; and Russell Targ, 83, 113, 116; and Anthony White, 113, 116

Delphic oracle, 74

Delta Force team, 93-94

Dennis, Eugenie: and David P. Abbott, 34; death of, 34; and Brighton trunk crime, 34, 36

Denton, William, 30-33

Detective work. *See* Psychic detection

Dior, Christian, 128

Diseases. *See* Sicknesses

Disney, Walt, 111
Displacement, 115
Divining Hand, The (Bird), 77
Dixon, Jeane, *9*, 10
Dogs: and psi-warfare experiments, 74, 76
Doshas, 98
Dowsing: and Elizabeth Albright, *127;* and Robert Brewer, *127;* and Paul Clement Brown, 128-130; equipment used in, *126, 127,* 128, 130; and Ian Fleming, 68, 69; and Harry Grattan, *126;* and Heinrich Himmler, 65; and Clayton McDowell, *126;* and Louis Matacia, 77; and mining, *122-123, 125,* 128-130; and Nazis, 59, 68; and psi-warfare experiments, 74, 77-78; and psychic detection, 27; and Vietcong tunnels, 77-78; and J. W. Young, 128. *See also* Map dowsing
Doyle, Arthur Conan, 29, *32-33*
Dozier, James, *92-93;* and Gary, 91-92; and Red Brigades, 91-92
Dream-telepathy research, 111. *See also* Telepathy
Dubček, Alexander, 13
Dunne, Brenda J., 88

E

Earthquakes: in Alaska, *10-11;* in San Francisco, 105
Ebertin, Elsbeth *(A Look into the Future), 58-59*
Eclipses, 123
Eiffel Tower, *89*
Eldridge, Tom, 47-48
Elements (Euclid), 118
ELF (extremely low frequency) waves, 86
Eliot, George, 30
Elisha (biblical figure), 73
Elizabeth I (queen of England), 74
Emerson, Ralph Waldo, 108
Emerson, Steven, 91
ESP: and Joseph A. Ball, 82; and Central Intelligence Agency, 85; and Brenda Dunn, 88; and Fadlallah, 93; and Elmar Gruber, 87; and Hella Hammid, 83; and Keith Harary, 113-115, 116; and Robert Jahn, 88; and Joel S. Lawson, Jr., 90; and Roger Nelson, 88; and Manuel Noriega, 92; and precognition, 113; and Joseph B. Rhine, 130; and Marilyn Schlitz, 87; and Stephan A. Schwartz, 89; and SRI International, 85; and stock market, 113, 115, 116; and Russell Targ, 81, 83, 89, 113; and *Taurus,* 82-83; and Anthony White, 113. *See also* Executive ESP; Intuition
Espionage. *See* Psi-warfare experiments
Evans, Mary Ann, 30
Executive ESP: and Weston Agor, 107, 130; and Douglas Dean, 107; and Conrad Hilton, 105; and Ray Kroc, 104-105; and Jesse Livermore, 105; and men vs. women, 107; and John Mihalasky, 107; and H. Ross Perot, 105; and precognition, 107, 130; and Sanyo Chemical Industries, Ltd., 107; and Anita Smith, 115; and Tarot, 115; and Masatoshi

Yoshimura, 107-108. *See also* ESP; Intuition
Extrasensory perception. *See* ESP
Extremely low frequency (ELF) waves, 86

F

Fadlallah (terrorist), 93
Faith healing, 95
Finke, Allen, 47
First Earth Battalion, 94
Fitzgerald, William: and Greta Alexander, 24, 25, 27; and Mary Cousett, 24, 25; quoted, 27
Flegenheimer, Arthur. *See* Schultz, Dutch
Fleming, Ian, *69;* and dowsing, 68, 69; and Nazis, 68; and submarines, 68, 69
F.L.Q. (Front de Liberation du Quebec): and James Jasper Cross, 41, 43; hideout of, *42;* and Pierre LaPorte, 41, 43
Foote, James, 82
Fortunetelling: and J. P. Morgan, 111; and Nazis, 59; and Cornelius Vanderbilt, 111. *See also* Precognition
Franciscan monk, *97*
Francis of Assisi, Saint, 97
Front de Liberation du Quebec. *See* F.L.Q.
Fuller, R. Buckminster, 108-109
Furstenberg, Diane von, 128

G

Gann, W. D., 118-119
Gary (psychic), 91-92
Geller, Uri: and John Aoki, 126; and clairvoyance, 124; and map dowsing, *122,* 124-126; and mining, *122-123;* and psychokinesis, 124; quoted, 124; and John Tishman, 126
Geller Effect, The (Geller), 124
Gestapo, 66. *See also* Nazis
Goebbels, Joseph, 62
Grail, 64
Grattan, Harry, *126*
Gruber, Elmar, 87
Gut feelings. *See* Executive ESP
Gutowski, Ace, 128

H

Hammid, Hella: and ESP, 83; quoted, 83; and SCANATE, 81; and *Taurus,* 83
Hand, Robert, *121*
Hanussen, Erik Jan, *60-61*
Harary, Keith: and Delphi Associates, 113, 116; and displacement, 115; and ESP, 113-115, 116; and Iran hostage crisis, 91; and National Security Council, 91; and precognition, 116-117; quoted, 115-116; and stock market, 113, 115, 116-117; and Russell Targ, 113-115; and Anthony White, 113
Harris, Susan, 86
Headwork, 94
Healing, and touch, *95-103*
Hearst, Patty: and Dorothy Allison, 43, 44; kidnapping of, 43, 44
Hearst, Randolph, 44
Heartwork, 94
Hejbalik, Karel, 74

Henry IV (king of France), *97*
Herodotus, 74
Hess, Rudolf, 64-65
Hickok, James Butler (Wild Bill), 77
Hilton, Conrad: and executive ESP, 105; and intuition, 109; quoted, 105; and Stevens Corporation, 105
Himmler, Heinrich, *64-65*
Hitler, Adolf, *58-59, 65;* and astrology, 64; and Beer Hall Putsch, 58, 62, *63;* and Elsbeth Ebertin, 58; and Rudolf Hess, 64, 65; and Heinrich Himmler, 64, 65; imprisonment of, 58; and Karl Ernst Krafft, 62; and Wolf Messing, 66; and Joseph Stalin, 66
Holliday, Stanley, Jr.: and Mary Cousett, 24, 26-27; murder conviction of, 27
Holy Grail, 64
Homing pigeons, 74
Horoscopes: by Hans Gerhard Lenz, 124; by Grace Morris, *118-119,* 123-124. *See also* Astrology
Hughes, Irene, 41-43
Hunches. *See* Executive ESP
Hunt, H. L., 111
Hurricane Agnes, *14-15*

I

Illnesses. *See* Sicknesses
Intuition: defined, 107, 108, 109; and Ralph Waldo Emerson, 108; and R. Buckminster Fuller, 108-109; and Conrad Hilton, 109; and William Kautz, 109, 110; and William W. Keeler, 109; and precognition, 109; and Roy Rowan, 130; and Baruch Spinoza, 108; and T. O. Tulley, 113; and Frances E. Vaughan, 107; and Masatoshi Yoshimura, 107-108. *See also* Clairvoyance; ESP; Executive ESP; Telepathy
Intuitive Management (Agor), 107
Intuitives. *See* Psychics
Ionospheric storms, 122
Iran hostage crisis, 91
Isaiah (spirit), 26

J

Jack the Ripper: and Robert James Lees, 27-29, 31; and psychic detection, 27-28; quoted, 31; and Scotland Yard, 27-29, 31; victims of, 27-28, *30-31*
Jaegers, Beverly, *20, 46;* and *Challenger* shuttle, 20; and *Columbia* shuttle, 20; and Fred Kolb, 20; and psychic detection, 45, 46, 48; and Psychic Detective Bureau, 45, 46, 48; and psychometry, 46; quoted, 20, 45, 48; and visualization, 46
Jahn, Robert, 88
Jin-Fa Zhang, *98*
Jones (lieutenant), 70-71
Jonsson, Olof, *112;* quoted, 112; and stock market, 112, 113

K

Kautz, William, *108-109;* and Center for Applied Intuition, 109, 130; and con-

sciousness, 109; and intuition, 109, 110; quoted, 109, 130; and super-conscious, 109
Kaye, Violette, residence of, *36*
Kazhinsky, Bernard *(Biological Radio Communications),* 79
Keeler, William W., 109
Kennedy, John F.: assassination of, *8-9,* 121; and Jeane Dixon, 9; presidential election of, 121; and David Williams, 121
King, Charlotte, *18*
King, George, 100
Kohlberg, Kravis, Roberts, 119
Kolb, Fred, 20
Krafft, Karl Ernst, *62-63*
Kroc, Ray, 104-105
Kulagina, Nina, 78

L

Laboratory of Biophysics, 84
Land mines: defined, 74; and dogs, 74, 76
LaPorte, Pierre, 41-43
Laurelite, 130
Lawson, Joel S., Jr., 90
Leaf, Horace: and Arthur Conan Doyle, 32; and psychometry, 32; quoted, 29
Leander (brig), *129;* and Mobius Society, 128; and Stephan A. Schwartz, 128
Lees, Robert James, *30-31;* and Jack the Ripper, 27-29, 31; and precognition, 27-28; and psychic detection, 27-29; and Scotland Yard, 27-28, 31; and spiritualism, 27; and Victoria, 27
Lenz, Hans Gerhard, *120-121;* and astroeconomics, 121, 124; and astrology, 124; horoscopes by, 124; quoted, 121, 124
Lewes, George Henry, 30
Lewis, Leslie, 126
Lightning: and Greta Alexander, 25, 26; and John Catchings, 49
Lily Dale Assembly, *28-29*
Linscott, Steve, 38-41
Livermore, Jesse, *110;* bankruptcy of, 112; death of, 112; and executive ESP, 105; and precognition, 110, 112; quoted, 111, 112; and stock market, 105, 111-112; and Union Pacific stock, 105, 111
Lorke, Gail, *52-53;* and John Catchings, 49-57; disappearance and murder of, 49, *57;* and Steven Lorke, 50, 53, *54-55,* 56; and square dancing, *50-51;* and Marty Wing, 50, 53, 56
Lorke, Steven: and Gail Lorke, 50, 53, *54-55,* 56; and Ronald Phillips, 56; quoted, 50; and Marty Wing, 50, 53, 56
Lorrain, Pierre Le, 27

M

McDonald, Maurice and Richard, 104-105
McDowell, Clayton, *126*
McRae, Ron: and Jack Anderson, 80; and Joel S. Lawson, Jr., 90; and psi-warfare experiments, 90; and Charles Rose, 80; and U.S. Navy, 90
Malibu Miniature Golf, 116-117

Mandlestam, Robert, 76
Manley, T. F., 77
Manual of Psychometry (Buchanan), 30
Map dowsing, and Uri Geller, *122,* 124-126. *See also* Dowsing
Mars-Jupiter Conjunction, 120
Matacia, Louis, 77
Matin de Magicien, Le (Bergier and Pauwels), 70, 71
Medicine Wolf (spirit), 77
Messadié, Gérald: and Jacques Bergier, 71; and *Nautilus,* 70; quoted, 71
Messing, Wolf, *66*
Mihalasky, John: and Douglas Dean, *106;* and executive ESP, 107; and plethysmograph, *106;* and precognition, 107; and telepathy, 106
Mind prints: and computers, 132; defined, 132; and neural networks, *132-133;* and quadriplegics, *136-137;* and RNGs, *132-133;* and telecommunications, *134-135*
Mind readers. *See* Psychics
Mind Wars (McRae), 82
Mining: and Paul Clement Brown, 128-130; and dowsing, *122-123, 125,* 128-130; and Uri Geller, *122-123;* and Clayton McDowell, *126;* and J. W. Young, 128
Mirror-image reversal, 17
Mobius Society: and *Leander,* 128; and parapsychology, 89; and Stephan A. Schwartz, 89, 128
Monk, Franciscan, *97*
Montgomery, Ruth, 18
Moore, James, 47
Morgan, J. P.: and Evangeline Adams, 120-121; and astrology, 120-121; and clairvoyance, 111; and fortunetelling, 111; and stock market, 121
Morris, Grace: and astro-economics, 118-119, 123-124; and astrology, 118-119, 123-124; horoscopes by, *118-119,* 123-124; and psychotherapy, 123; quoted, 124; and stock market, 123; and World Conference of Astro-Economics, 124
Mountain men, 77
Multispectral image analyzer station, 84-90
Muscle reading, 27
Mussolini, Benito, 65
Myers, Frederic W. H., 27

N

Nash, John A., 34
Natal charts, *118-119*
National Security Council (NSC), 91
Natural Law of Vibration, 119
Naumov, Eduard, *80;* imprisonment of, 80, 84; at Laboratory of Biophysics, 84; and *Nautilus,* 79; and parapsychology, 79; and Valery G. Petukhov, 84; and psi-warfare experiments, 84; and telepathy, 79
Nautilus (submarine), *72-73;* and William Anderson, 71; and Jacques Bergier, 71,

72; and William Bowers, 71; and Lieutenant Jones, 70-71; and Gérald Messadié, 70; and Eduard Naumov, 79; and psi-warfare experiments, 72, 78; and Smith, 70; and Soviet Union, 71-72, 79; and telepathy, 70-71; and Leonid Vasiliev, 78. *See also* Submarines
Navy, U.S., 84-90
Nazis: and astrology, *69;* and Beer Hall Putsch, 58; and dowsing, 59, 68; and Ian Fleming, 68; and fortunetelling, 59; and Erik Jan Hanussen, *60-61;* and Stefan Ossowiecki, 66, 67; and psi powers, 58-69; and psi-warfare experiments, *68-69. See also* SS
Nelson, Roger, 88
Nerve auras, 30
Neural networks: defined, 132; and mind prints, *132-133;* and quadriplegics, *136-137;* and telecommunications, *134-135*
"New Mental Battlefield, The" (J. Alexander), 90-91
Nkrumah, Kwame, 76
Nolan, Finbarr, *103*
Noriega, Manuel, 92
Nostradamus: and Joseph Goebbels, 62; and Karl Ernst Krafft, 62, *63;* and Louis de Wohl, 68
NSC, 91
Numerology, 75

O

Operational Thetans, 84
Oracle of Delphi, *74*
Ossowiecki, Stefan, *67;* and Nazis, 66, 67
Out-of-body travel: and Church of Scientology, 84; and Ingo Swann, 85; and warrior-monks, 94

P

Palace of the Occult, and Erik Jan Hanussen, 60, *61*
Palitayan, Placido, *102;* quoted, 103
Palmer, Nelson, *39;* and Myrna Joy Aken, 35-36, 37, 39; and psychic detection, 35, 39; and psychometry, 35-36, 37, 39; quoted, 36; and Clarence Van Buuren, 37
Parapsychology: and Central Intelligence Agency, 80, 91; and Mobius Society, 89; and Eduard Naumov, 79; and psi-warfare experiments, 79; and Charles Rose, 80; and Soviet Union, 78-79
Paris, France, *62-63*
Perkins, Joseph, 45
Perot, H. Ross, 105
Persian Gulf war, 111
Petukhov, Valery G., 84
Phillips, Karen, 38-40
Phillips, Ronald, 56
Pigeons, 74
Plethysmograph, *106*
Practical ESP and Clairvoyance (Jaegers), 46
Prague, Czechoslovakia, *12-13*
Precognition: and Weston Agor, 130; and

Douglas Dean, 107; defined, 7, 25; and ESP, 113; examples of, *8-23;* and executive ESP, 107, 130; and Keith Harary, 116-117; and intuition, 109; and William W. Keeler, 109; and Robert James Lees, 27-28; and Jesse Livermore, 110, 112; and John Mihalasky, 107; and mirror-image reversal, 17; and Harold Puthoff, 83; and stock market, 113, 115, 116-117; and Russell Targ, 83; and Alan Vaughan, 14. *See also* Fortunetelling
Price, Pat, 81-82, 84
Psi powers: and computers, 131; and Nazis, 58-69; and psychic detection, 7; and telecommunications, *134-135;* types of, 7
Psi Squad. *See* Psychic Detective Bureau
Psi Tech, 90
Psi-warfare experiments: and Joseph A. Ball, 82; and Jacques Bergier, 72; in Bible, 73; and Britain, *68-69;* and Central Intelligence Agency, 76, 79, 80, 81-82; and clairvoyance, 7; criticism of, 94; and John Dee, 74; and Delta Force team, 93-94; and dogs, 74, 76; and dowsing, 74, *77-78;* and Fadlallah, 93; and First Earth Battalion, 94; and Karel Hejbalik, 74; and homing pigeons, 74; and Iran hostage crisis, 91; and Ron McRae, 90; and Eduard Naumov, 84; and *Nautilus,* 72, 78; and Nazis, *68-69;* and Manuel Noriega, 92; and parapsychology, 79; and Psi Tech, 90; purposes of, *72-73;* and qi, 73; and Ronald Reagan, 91; and Zdeněk Rejdák, 74; and Joseph Rhine, 74-76; and Soviet Union, 78, 79-80, 84; and SRI International, 80-83, 91; and *Taurus,* 82-83; and U.S. Navy, 84-90; and Winter Harvest, 91-92; and Madame Zodiac, 90
Psiwork, 94
Psychic detection: and Greta Alexander, 24-27; and Dorothy Allison, 43-44; and astrology, 27; in Bible, 27; and George Brejack, 44; and John Catchings, 49-57; and Donald Cherry, 40; criticism of and praise for, 44-45; and crystal balls, 27; and Nancy Czetli, 45-47; and Eugenie Dennis, 34; and dowsing, 27; and Arthur Conan Doyle, 29, 32; and Irene Hughes, 42, 43; and Jack the Ripper, 27-28; and Beverly Jaegers, 45, 46, 48; and Robert James Lees, 27-29; and Steve Linscott, 38-41; and muscle reading, 27; and Nelson Palmer, 35, 39; and Joseph Perkins, 45; and psi powers, 7; and Psychic Detective Bureau, 45, 46; and psychometry, 29-30, 32, 33; and James Randi, 44-45; and Scotland Yard, 27; and Etta Louise Smith, 37-38; and Florence Sternfels, 33-34; and Dixie Yeterian, 47
Psychic Detective Bureau, *46;* and Beverly Jaegers, 45, 46, 48; and psychic detection, 45, 46; and psychometry, 46; purposes of, 48
Psychic healing, and touch, *95-103*

Psychics: characteristics of, 24-25, 37, 41; criticism of, 25, 37, 41; exercises for, 46. *See also specific psychics*
Psychic split, 48
Psychic spying. *See* Psi-warfare experiments
Psychokinesis: characteristics of, 134; and computers, 131; and Uri Geller, 124; and Dean Radin, 131; and Joseph B. Rhine, 130
Psychological warfare. *See* Psi-warfare experiments
Psychometry, *33;* and Joseph Rodes Buchanan, 30; defined, 7, 29, 30, 33; and William Denton, 30-33; and Arthur Conan Doyle, 29; and Beverly Jaegers, 46; and Horace Leaf, 32; and George Henry Lewes, 30; and nerve auras, 30; and Nelson Palmer, 35-36, 37, 39; psychic detection, 29-30, 32, 33; and Psychic Detective Bureau, 46; purposes of, 46; and Florence Sternfels, 33; and telepathy, 30; and Dixie Yeterian, 47-48
Psychotherapy, 123
Psychotronic equipment, 84
Psychotronics: and John B. Alexander, 90-91; conference on, *81;* and Zdeněk Rejdák, 80, *81;* and Soviet Union, 90-91
Puthoff, Harold: and Central Intelligence Agency, 81; and Church of Scientology, 84; and clairvoyance, 80; and ELF waves, 86; photograph by, *86;* and precognition, 83; and Pat Price, 81-82; quoted, 80-81, 84; and SRI International, 81, 83; and Ingo Swann, 85; and John Wilhelm, 84

Q

Qi: defined, 73, 98; and psi-warfare experiments, 73; and Sun Tzu, 73
Qigong therapy, *98*
Quadriplegics, *136-137*
Queen, Richard, 91

R

Radin, Dean, *131*
Railway Workers' House of Culture, *81*
Randi, James, 44-45
Random bits, 131
Random number generators. *See* RNGs
Raoul (spirit), 26
Red Brigades, 91-92
Reichstag: burning of, *60;* and Erik Jan Hanussen, 60, 61
Rejdák, Zdeněk, *81;* and psi-warfare experiments, 74; and psychotronics, 80
Remote viewing. *See* ESP
Retrocognition, 7
Reverse connection, 103
Rhine, Joseph B.: and dogs, 76; and ESP, 130; and psi-warfare experiments, 74-76; and psychokinesis, 130; quoted, 130
Richardson, George F., 33
RNGs (random number generators): and mind prints, *132-133;* and quadriplegics, *136-137;* and telecommunications, *134-135. See also* T7001

Roark, Ronald, 49
Robbins, Shawn: and advertising campaigns, 127; quoted, 113, 127; and stock market, 113; visions of, 127-128
Romanos, Del, 48
Rome International Airport, *87*
Rose, Charles, 80
Rowan, Roy, 130
Ryan, Lee, 37

S

Saint Helens, Mount, *18-19*
Samuel (biblical figure), and Saul, 27, *29*
San Andrés Island, *86*
San Francisco earthquake, 105
Sanyo Chemical Industries, Ltd., 107
Saul (biblical figure), and Samuel, 27, *29*
SCANATE, 81-82
Schilling, Leonetta, 46-47
Schlitz, Marilyn, 87
Schultz, Dutch: murder of, 33, *35;* and Florence Sternfels, 33, 35
Schwartz, Stephan A., *129;* and ESP, 89; and *Leander*, 128; and Mobius Society, 89, 128
Science Unlimited Research Foundation (SURF), 81
Scientology, 84
Scotland Yard: and Agatha Christie, 29; and Jack the Ripper, 27-29, 31; and Robert James Lees, 27-28, 31; and psychic detection, 27
Scrofula, 95
Séances, and Erik Jan Hanussen, 60, *61*
Sensitives. See Psychics
"Shew stones." See Crystal balls
Sicknesses: causes of, 95; curing of, 90, *95-103;* and multispectral image analyzer station, 90
Sixth sense. See Executive ESP
Skillen, Robert, 90
Slipping the silver lining, 94
Smith (telepathic sender), 70
Smith, Anita, *114-115*
Smith, Etta Louise, 37-38
Soviet Union: and ELF waves, 86; and *Nautilus*, 71-72, 79; and parapsychology, 78-79; and psi-warfare experiments, 78, 79-80, 84; and psychotronics, 90-91; and telepathy, 78, 79
Spinoza, Baruch, 108
Spiritualism, *28-29;* background of, 27; and Arthur Conan Doyle, 32; and Robert James Lees, 27
Spying. See Psi-warfare experiments
SRI International: and Joseph A. Ball, 82; and Central Intelligence Agency, 81-82, 83, 85; and Church of Scientology, 84; and clairvoyance, 80; criticism of, 83-84; and ESP, 85; and Iran hostage crisis, 91; and Pat Price, 82; and psi-warfare

experiments, 80-83, 91; and Harold Puthoff, 81, 83; and SCANATE, 81-82; and Science Unlimited Research Foundation, 81; and Ingo Swann, 85; and Russell Targ, 81, 83, 94; and *Taurus*, 82-83
SS, 64. See also Nazis
Stalin, Joseph, 66
Stanford Research Institute. See SRI International
State Control Institute of Medical Biological Preparations, 84
Steinschneider, Hermann, *60-61*
Sternfels, Florence: and Hereward Carrington, 34; death of, 34; and John A. Nash, 34; and psychic detection, 33-34; and psychometry, 33; quoted, 33, 34; and George F. Richardson, 33; and Dutch Schultz, 33, 35
Stevens Corporation, 105
Stock market: and astro-economics, 118; and astrology, *118-119*, 120; and Malcolm Bessent, 111; and Delphi Associates, 113, 115, 116-117; and ESP, 113, 115, 116; and W. D. Gann, 118-119; and Keith Harary, 113, 115, 116-117; and Olof Jonsson, 112, 113; and Jesse Livermore, 105, 111-112; and Mars-Jupiter Conjunction, 120; and J. P. Morgan, 121; and Grace Morris, 123; and Natural Law of Vibration, 119; and precognition, 113, 115, 116-117; and Shawn Robbins, 113; and Anita Smith, 115; and sunspots, 119-120, 122; and Russell Targ, 113, 115, 116-117; and Tarot, 115, 116, 117; and Marty Tressler, 116-117; and T. O. Tulley, 113; and Anthony White, 113, 115, 116-117; and David Williams, 119, 120-121; and witches, 117
Stock market crash (1929): and Evangeline Adams, 121; and astrology, 120. See also Black Tuesday
Stock market crash (1987), 123
Storms, ionospheric, 122
Sturtz, Roseanne Michele, *40-41*
Submarines: and Ian Fleming, 68, 69; and multispectral image analyzer station, 84-90; sinking of, *68-69;* and telecommunications, *134-135;* and Madame Zodiac, 90. See also *Nautilus; Taurus*
Sukarno, Achmed, 76-77
Sunspots: and Arch Crawford, 122; and stock market, 119-120, 122; and David Williams, 119-120
Sun Tzu *(The Art of War)*, 73
Super-conscious: defined, 109; and William Kautz, 109; and Masatoshi Yoshimura, 108, 109-110
SURF, 81
Swann, Ingo, *23, 85;* and Berlin Wall, 23; and Central Intelligence Agency, 85;

and Church of Scientology, 84; and Iran hostage crisis, 91; and National Security Council, 91; and out-of-body travel, 85; and Harold Puthoff, 85; quoted, 23, 82, 83, 85; and SCANATE, 81, 82; and SRI International, 85; and Russell Targ, 85; and *Taurus*, 83; and John Wilhelm, 84

T

Targ, Russell: and Central Intelligence Agency, 81; and Church of Scientology, 84; and clairvoyance, 80, 81; and Delphi Associates, 83, 113, 116; and ELF waves, 86; and ESP, 81, 83, 89, 113; and Keith Harary, 113-115; and precognition, 83; quoted, 81, 89; and SRI International, 81, 83, 94; and stock market, 113, 115, 116-117; and Ingo Swann, 85; and *Taurus*, 83; and Anthony White, 113, 115
Tarot: and executive ESP, 115; and Anita Smith, *114-115;* and stock market, 115, 116, 117
Taurus (submarine), 82-83. See also Submarines
Technical remote viewing, 90. See also ESP
Telecommunications, *134-135*
Telekinesis, 78
Telepathy: and Church of Scientology, 84; and Douglas Dean, 106; defined, 25, 27; and William Denton, 30; and Lieutenant Jones, 70-71; and Bernard Kazhinsky, 79; and John Mihalasky, 106; and Frederic W. H. Myers, 27; and Eduard Naumov, 79; and *Nautilus*, 70-71; and Valery G. Petukhov, 84; and psychometry, 30; and Smith, 70; and Soviet Union, 78, 79; and T. O. Tulley, 113; and Leonid Vasiliev, 78. See also Dream-telepathy research; Intuition
Thatcher, Margaret, 111
Tishman, John, 126
Toth, Robert, 84
Touch, and psychic healing, *95-103*
Toušek, Milan, *13*
Tressler, Marty, 116-117
Trew, Steve, 26
T7001, 131. See also RNGs
Tulley, T. O., 113
Tunnels, Vietcong, *77-78*

U

Union of Soviet Socialist Republics. See Soviet Union
Union Pacific stock, and Jesse Livermore, 105, 111
United Kingdom, and psi-warfare experiments, *68-69*
U.S. Navy, 84-90
Uranium, 130

and Church of Scientology, 84; and Iran hostage crisis, 91; and National Security Council, 91; and out-of-body travel, 85; and Harold Puthoff, 85; quoted, 23, 82, 83, 85; and SCANATE, 81, 82; and SRI International, 85; and Russell Targ, 85; and *Taurus*, 83; and John Wilhelm, 84

Uribe, Melanie: disappearance and murder of, 37, 38; and Etta Louise Smith, 37
Urquardt Castle, *88*
USSR. See Soviet Union

V

Van Buuren, Clarence, *39;* and Myrna Joy Aken, 36-37, 39; and Nelson Palmer, 37
Vanderbilt, Cornelius, 111
Vasiliev, Leonid *(Experiments in Distant Influence)*, 78
Vaughan, Alan, *14*
Vaughan, Frances E., 107
Victoria (queen of United Kingdom), 27
Vietcong tunnels, 77-78
Visions: of Elisha, 73; of Karl Ernst Krafft, 63; of Shawn Robbins, 127-128
Visualization, 46

W

Wadley, J. K., 128-130
Wall Street and Witchcraft (Gunther), 111, 113, 116-118
Warrior-monks, 94
Warsaw, Poland, *66-67*
Wewelsburg Castle, *64*
White, Anthony: and Delphi Associates, 113, 116; and ESP, 113; and Keith Harary, 113; and stock market, 113, 115, 116-117; and Russell Targ, 113, 115
Whitehouse, Charles, 84-90
Wilhelm, John, 82, 84
Wilkes-Barre, Pennsylvania, *14-15*
Williams, David: and astrology, 119; and John F. Kennedy, 121; and Mars-Jupiter Conjunction, 120; quoted, 120; and stock market, 119, 120-121; and sunspots, 119-120
Williams, Wayne, 44
Wing, Marty: and John Catchings, 53, 56; and Gail and Steven Lorke, 50, 53, 56; and Ronald Phillips, 56
Winter Harvest, 91-92
Wise women. See Psychics
Witches, *29;* and stock market, 117
Wohl, Louis de, *68*
World Conference of Astro-Economics, 124

Y

Yeterian, Dixie, 47-48
Yolana (psychic), 128
Yoshimura, Masatoshi: and executive ESP, 107-108; and super-conscious, 108, 109-110
Young, J. W., 128

Z

Zodiac, Madame, 90

TIME-LIFE BOOKS

EDITOR-IN-CHIEF: John L. Papanek

Executive Editor: Roberta Conlan
Director of Editorial Resources: Elise D. Ritter-Clough
Executive Art Director: Ellen Robling
Director of Photography and Research: John Conrad Weiser
Editorial Board: Russell B. Adams, Jr., Dale M. Brown, Janet Cave, Robert Doyle, Jim Hicks, Rita Thievon Mullin, Robert Somerville, Henry Woodhead
Assistant Director of Editorial Resources: Norma E. Shaw

PRESIDENT: John D. Hall

Vice President, Director of Marketing: Nancy K. Jones
Vice President, New Product Development: Neil Kagan
Director of Production Services: Robert N. Carr
Production Manager: Marlene Zack
Director of Technology: Eileen Bradley
Supervisor of Quality Control: James King

Editorial Operations
Production: Celia Beattie
Library: Louise D. Forstall
Computer Composition: Deborah G. Tait (Manager), Monika D. Thayer, Janet Barnes Syring, Lillian Daniels
Interactive Media Specialist: Patti H. Cass

Time-Life Books is a division of Time Life Inc.

PRESIDENT AND CEO: John M. Fahey, Jr.

Library of Congress Cataloging in Publication Data
The psychics / by the editors of Time-Life Books.
  p. cm.—(Mysteries of the unknown)
  ISBN 0-8094-6542-6 (library)
  ISBN 0-8094-6541-8 (trade)
  1. Psychics. 2. Parapsychology—Military aspects.
3. Parapsychology and business.
  I. Time-Life Books.   II. Series.
BF1040.P76 1992
133.8—dc20   92-3147
                                                  CIP

MYSTERIES OF THE UNKNOWN

SERIES EDITOR: Jim Hicks
Series Administrators: Barbara Levitt, Jane A. Martin
Art Director: Tom Huestis
Picture Editor: Paula York-Soderlund

Editorial Staff for *The Psychics*
Text Editors: Janet Cave (principal), Esther Ferington
Associate Editor/Research: Christian D. Kinney
Assistant Editor/Research: Dan Kulpinski
Assistant Art Directors: Susan M. Gibas, Brook Mowrey, Lorraine D. Rivard
Writers: Charles J. Hagner, Sarah D. Ince
Copy Coordinators: Donna Carey, Juli Duncan
Picture Coordinators: David Herod, Julia Kendrick
Editorial Assistant: Donna Fountain

Special Contributors: Patty U. Chang, Mimi Fallow, Barbara Fleming, Patricia A. Paterno, Evelyn S. Prettyman, Nancy J. Seeger (research); Margery A. duMond, Marfé Ferguson Delano, Lydia Preston Hicks, Harvey Loomis, Susan Perry, Peter W. Pocock, Daniel Stashower (text); John Drummond (design); Marcello Truzzi, Alan Vaughan (consultants); Hazel Blumberg-McKee (index).

Correspondents: Elisabeth Kraemer-Singh (Bonn), Christine Hinze (London), Christina Lieberman (New York), Maria Vincenza Aloisi (Paris), Ann Natanson (Rome).
Valuable assistance was also provided by: Angelika Lemmer (Bonn); Peter Hawthorne (Capetown); Bing Wong (Hong Kong); Judy Aspinall (London); Juan Sosa (Moscow); Elizabeth Brown, Katheryn White (New York); Michal Donath (Prague); Leonora Dodsworth, Ann Wise, (Rome); Traudl Lessing (Vienna).

Other Publications:

THE WEIGHT WATCHERS® SMART CHOICE
  RECIPE COLLECTION
TRUE CRIME
THE AMERICAN INDIANS
THE ART OF WOODWORKING
LOST CIVILIZATIONS
ECHOES OF GLORY
THE NEW FACE OF WAR
HOW THINGS WORK
WINGS OF WAR
CREATIVE EVERYDAY COOKING
COLLECTOR'S LIBRARY OF THE UNKNOWN
CLASSICS OF WORLD WAR II
TIME-LIFE LIBRARY OF CURIOUS AND UNUSUAL FACTS
AMERICAN COUNTRY
VOYAGE THROUGH THE UNIVERSE
THE THIRD REICH
THE TIME-LIFE GARDENER'S GUIDE
TIME FRAME
FIX IT YOURSELF
FITNESS, HEALTH & NUTRITION
SUCCESSFUL PARENTING
HEALTHY HOME COOKING
UNDERSTANDING COMPUTERS
LIBRARY OF NATIONS
THE ENCHANTED WORLD
THE KODAK LIBRARY OF CREATIVE PHOTOGRAPHY
GREAT MEALS IN MINUTES
THE CIVIL WAR
PLANET EARTH
COLLECTOR'S LIBRARY OF THE CIVIL WAR
THE EPIC OF FLIGHT
THE GOOD COOK
WORLD WAR II
HOME REPAIR AND IMPROVEMENT
THE OLD WEST

For information on and a full description of any of the Time-Life Books series listed above, please call 1-800-621-7026 or write:
Reader Information
Time-Life Customer Service
P.O. Box C-32068
Richmond, Virginia 23261-2068

This volume is one of a series that examines the history and nature of seemingly paranormal phenomena. Other books in the series include:

Mystic Places   *Witches and Witchcraft*
Psychic Powers   *Time and Space*
The UFO Phenomenon   *Magical Arts*
Psychic Voyages   *Utopian Visions*
Phantom Encounters   *Secrets of the Alchemists*
Visions and Prophecies   *Eastern Mysteries*
Mysterious Creatures   *Earth Energies*
Mind over Matter   *Cosmic Duality*
Cosmic Connections   *Mysterious Lands and Peoples*
Spirit Summonings   *The Mind and Beyond*
Ancient Wisdom   *Mystic Quests*
  and Secret Sects   *Search for Immortality*
Hauntings   *The Mystical Year*
Powers of Healing   *Alien Encounters*
Search for the Soul   *The Mysterious World*
Transformations   *Master Index*
Dreams and Dreaming   *and Illustrated Symbols*